We Are Baptists

We Are Baptists
Studies for Youth

Jeffrey D. Jones and Debra L. Sutton

Judson Press
Valley Forge

We Are Baptists: Studies for Youth
© 1999 by Judson Press, Valley Forge, PA 19482-0851
All rights reserved.

Unless otherwise indicated Bible quotations in this volume are from The New Revised Standard Version of the Bible, copyright © 1989 by the Division of Christian Education of the National Council of the Churches of Christ in the United States of America. Used by permission. All rights reserved.

Bible quotations designated CEV are from the Contemporary English Version. © 1991, 1995 American Bible Society. Used by permission.

Bible quotations designated TEV are from the *Good News Bible: Today's English Version*. Copyright © American Bible Society 1966, 1971, 1992. Used by permission.

The writers wish to acknowledge the work of Ron Arena for the sessions "The Bible" and "Priesthood of Believers" and John Fischer for the session on "Evangelism."

Library of Congress Cataloging-in-Publication Data

Jones, Jeffrey D.
  We Are Baptists: studies for youth / Jeffrey D. Jones and Debra L. Sutton.
     p.   cm.
  Includes bibliographical references.
  ISBN 0-8170-1322-9 (pbk. : alk. paper)
     1. Baptists—Education   2. Christian education of teenagers.   I. Sutton, Debra L.   II. Title.
  BX6225.J66 1999
  268'.433—dc21   99-12952

Printed in the U.S.A.
06   05   04   03   02   01   00   99
10   9   8   7   6   5   4   3   2   1

Contents

Ways to Use This Curriculum

We Are Baptists is a flexible curriculum. One way it can be used is for a six-week program to establish a foundational understanding of what it means to be Baptist—ideal for youth seeking to make a decision about baptism. We suggest using the first six lessons for this shorter, focused study: Soul Freedom, Believer's Baptism, The Bible, Priesthood of All Believers, Religious Liberty, and Autonomy of the Local Church. For a more in-depth study, use all fourteen sessions for an entire quarter on what it means to be Baptist. Still other ways to use these materials include:

- Sunday church school
- a church-wide celebration of Baptist heritage
- a weekly family night program or other special gatherings for youth and adults
- a Baptist heritage retreat

However you choose to use these lessons, they are designed for congregations wishing to learn more about Baptist identity and beliefs. Each session addresses a single theme, which is biblically rooted, as a way of helping to define who Baptists are and what they believe and do. It is our hope that leaders and learners will grow in their understanding of denominational heritage and the contributions Baptists have made and continue to make in today's world.

Preparing for each session is an important part of the teaching process. Become familiar with the session objectives and outline prior to each lesson. Since you know the youth with whom you are working, you can decide how to adapt the material to fit their needs and interests. Less lecture and more involvement in the learning process usually works best with youth. Be creative!

A few sessions require special materials; however, the following materials are needed for each session:

- Bibles
- a copy of the lesson handout for each youth
- pens or pencils
- newsprint and markers or chalkboard and chalk

1

Soul Freedom
Who Do You Say Jesus Is?

Bible Basis:
Matthew 16:13–16

Objectives

At the end of the session youth will be able to:

- explain the meaning of soul freedom;
- describe at least one way they will use that freedom to grow in their relationship with Christ.

Key Bible Verse:

"'Who do you say that I am?'" (Matthew 16:15).

Background for the Leader

Soul freedom. To our ears those words may sound odd. Yet they lie at the very heart of what makes us Baptists. Our belief in believer's baptism, in religious liberty, in the priesthood of believers—all the fundamental Baptist emphases—rests on the foundation of soul freedom. Simply put, it is the right and responsibility of each person to stand before God and make decisions about his or her relationship with God. Only when one has done this can the commitment of believer's baptism be made. Thus, religious liberty is essential. And living in this freedom, we become priests to one another.

Rightly understood, soul freedom is not rampant individualism, although it puts great emphasis on the individual. Rather, it is placing oneself in the hands of God, sometimes through the community of faith, sometimes all alone, but always submitting to God's will. The purpose of this session is to explore this some-

what odd, sometimes unfamiliar, but always important foundational principle of our Baptist beliefs.

"Our key is this: To understand the Baptists we must see the principle called 'soul freedom.' By this we mean the deep conviction that every man or woman has both the ability and the necessity to enter into direct saving relationship to God through Christ. Baptists believe that this is a personal relationship needing no outside mediation or formation."[1] These are the words seminary and American Baptist Churches in the U.S.A. president Gene Bartlett uses to introduce Baptists to those who might not know us very well. If you want to understand us, he seems to be saying, you need to understand soul freedom. As true as that is, it is also true that many Baptists would be at a loss to describe soul freedom and the way in which it has shaped our life together as a denomination.

The word *soul* is particularly difficult. Its meaning today seems limited to the *religious* aspect of a person. When Baptists first began to talk about soul freedom, however, soul meant much more. They understood it to mean the very core of our being, that central part of us that provides the true essence of who we are as persons. Early Baptists maintained that the core is free—not that it should be free and not that there should be laws guaranteeing its freedom, but that it *is* free. God created each of us with a free soul. In this freedom individuals develop a relationship with their Creator and discover whom God intended them to be.

Soul freedom isn't license to do anything or be anybody. Rather, it is the freedom to discover and respond to God's call in one's life, the freedom to find and follow God's will and way. Baptists have always recognized that this is something no one can determine for or dictate to another. Bartlett describes two implications of soul freedom for Baptists: "Believing in freedom of soul as the essential truth of the Christian life, Baptists historically have moved on two fronts of religious experience. (1) They have resisted anything which seemed to them oppression of freedom of soul. (2) They have insisted on anything which seemed the expression of the freedom."[2] Soul freedom leads us to resist government involvement in religion so that each person is free to pray or not and in any manner he or she chooses. Soul freedom leads us to insist on congregational government so that there is no hierarchy imposing its will or its understanding of God's truth upon others.

Thus, belief in soul freedom explains our lack of reliance on creeds. It explains the diversity that exists within and among Baptist churches and denominations. Its practice in our congregational and denominational life is also what permits the Holy Spirit to work in our midst, to open new possibilities for us, to lead us into new ways of being and doing, into new ways of faithfulness.

Working all of this out in a context of differing values, divergent understandings of God's will, and different interpretations of God's Word is always difficult. There are no set answers. Even today the attempt to do this creates intense conversations, sometimes even conflict, within Baptist churches and denominations. The principle remains, however. Soul freedom is at the very core of what it means to be a Baptist. It is a heritage we must both celebrate and protect.

Exploring the Biblical Basis

Jesus knew the end was near. His Galilean ministry of teaching and healing was drawing to a close and he was about to begin his journey to Jerusalem—and death. It was time for decisiveness, both in his own teaching and in what he asked of his disciples. He began gently. "Who do people say that I am?" He undoubtedly knew the answer, for he had heard the gossip: "He's a prophet come back to life—maybe John the Baptist, or Elijah, or Jeremiah." The disciples reported accurately. It was what they had heard too. All this was safe enough. It's always easy to talk about what others think, what others believe. But then Jesus pushed them. "Who do *you* say that I am?" he asked. Now he had gotten personal. Jesus was asking for an "I statement."

Jesus knew that all the teaching, healing, and casting out of demons he had done was worthless unless they understood that it was more than God-talk, more than making people healthy, more than battles over rules and regulations of the faith. They needed to understand that Jesus was the Messiah, the one for whom they had been waiting, and that God was intervening in human history to offer people new life in God's kingdom.

Jesus couldn't force this truth on his disciples; they had to get it on their own. Confessing him to be the Christ must be their decision, made in full freedom, for that was the only way it would really be their faith—a faith they would commit themselves to, even to death. That was the only way. It still is.

The Gospel writers didn't know the term *soul freedom*, but they wrote about it. Despite ridicule and rejection, the woman came to Jesus to pour perfume on him and wash his feet with her hair. That is soul freedom. The rich young man turned away because he wasn't willing to do what was needed to follow Jesus. That, too, is soul freedom.

Biblical examples of soul freedom go all the way back to the first chapter of Genesis when human beings were created in God's image. It is the freedom abused in the eating of the fruit. It is the freedom lived out in the faithful obedience of Abraham and Sarah, in the suffering of Jeremiah. Each one in full freedom, freedom granted by God, stood before God and decided. Each one in full freedom said yes or no to the call of God in his or her life. That is what soul freedom is all about.

Soul freedom was at work in Peter too. Jesus asked Peter, "Who do *you* say that I am?" In full freedom, from the depth of his being, with his very soul, Peter replied, "You are the Messiah, the Son of the living God." Praise be to God!

As you prepare for this lesson:

Pray for each youth by name. Today's session is about soul freedom, which is an important issue for youth, since they are at a point in their personal development where they desire greater freedom in their lives and are learning to accept and follow through on the responsibility that goes with that freedom. The focus of this session is to help them understand the freedom God gave them and to accept the responsibility of developing their relationship with Christ within that freedom. Reflect on and pray for each member of your class. Think about where he or she is in this important process. Pray that the class session will help your students meet the challenges and responsibilities that come with the soul freedom they have.

Read and reflect on the Bible passage. This session's Bible passage is a familiar one.

As you read it, put yourself in Peter's place. Who do the youth you know say that Jesus is? Think below the surface so that you consider what they are really saying, not just the words they speak. Then consider your own reply to Jesus' question, "Who do you say that I am?" Again, move beyond the words of your response to the way you live. As you do this, become more fully aware, not only of the great freedom we have in our relationship with God, but also of the great responsibility.

Beginning

1. **Who Jesus is.** (5–10 minutes)
   - Before the youth arrive, place three large sheets of newsprint around the room. Title the first sheet: "Who do your parents say Jesus is?" Title the second: "Who do your friends say Jesus is?" Title the third: "Who do you say Jesus is?"
   - Welcome the youth as they arrive.
   - Ask them to walk around the room and write words or phrases in response to the question on each list.
   - After several minutes, ask them to sit down and review the lists together.
   - Ask: "What similarities and/or differences do you see among the three lists?"

Exploring

2. **Bible reflection.** (5 minutes)
   - Ask the youth to turn to Matthew 16:13–16 in their Bibles.
   - Tell them that this passage asks the same questions you have been looking at: Who do people say Jesus is? Who do you say Jesus is?
   - Ask a volunteer to read the passage aloud as the others follow along.
   - Explain to the class that Jesus, in asking these questions, assumes that each person is free to decide who he is.
   - Ask: "What in this passage illustrates freedom?" (*One sign that we have freedom to decide about Jesus is that different*

people make different decisions. The material in "Exploring the Biblical Basis" provides additional information you may want to use at this point.)

3. **The meaning of soul freedom.**
(10 minutes)
   - Explain that Baptists have traditionally used the term *soul freedom* to describe this kind of freedom.
   - Write the words *soul freedom* on the chalkboard or newsprint. *(Acknowledge that these words may sound a bit odd to us because they come from an earlier time in our history, but their meaning is still very significant.)*
   - Distribute handout #1.
   - Ask the youth to look at "Soul Freedom."
   - Read the first paragraph aloud in unison.
   - Divide the class into three groups.
   - Assign each group one of the next three paragraphs.
   - Instruct each group to read and summarize their paragraph for the entire class.
   - After 3–4 minutes bring the class back together to share the summaries.
   - As the summaries are shared, write the key words on newsprint or chalkboard: *religious freedom, believer's baptism, no creeds, no bishops, congregational autonomy.*
   - Use the material in "Background for the Leader" to expand briefly on these important points.

4. **How others respond to Jesus.**
(10–15 minutes)
   - Ask youth to locate "Others Respond to Jesus" on the handout.
   - Divide the class into four groups.
   - Assign one passage to each group.
   - Ask each group to read its assigned passage and discuss the way in which the passage illustrates soul freedom.
   - After 5 minutes bring the groups back together.
   - Ask each group to share the way in

which the passage illustrates soul freedom. *(Important points from these passages include: people make different decisions about Jesus, and Jesus always allows them the freedom to decide even if they decide not to follow him.)*

5. **The responsibilities of soul freedom.**
(10–15 minutes)
   - Briefly make these key points:
     - Soul freedom gives each one of us both the right *and the responsibility* to develop our relationship with God.
     - The purpose of this freedom is that each one of us will discover God's will and way for his or her own life.
   - Ask someone in the class to read "Rights and Responsibilities" from the handout.
   - Facilitate a discussion using these or your own questions:
     1. What specific responsibilities do you think are involved in soul freedom?
     2. Since soul freedom is the freedom to develop our relationship with God, what do we need to do in order to do that?
     3. How do we discover God's will and way for our lives?
     4. Once we discover God's will and way for our lives, what responsibility do we have to follow them?
     5. How do we do that? What if we fail?
     6. If we can exercise this soul freedom better when there is religious liberty, what can we do to help to maintain separation of church and state?
   - Work with the class to complete the "Soul Freedom Declaration" in the handout.

Responding

6. **The declaration and prayer.** (5 minutes)
   - Ask the youth to read their "Soul Freedom Declaration" together.

- Using a "popcorn" style of prayer, invite the youth to pray. Going last, thank God for creating us with the freedom to develop our relationship with Christ. Ask for the insight and courage to do that faithfully.

(Note: If the youth agree, you might consider printing their declaration in the church newsletter as a way of making others aware of this important Baptist principle.)

Notes

1. Gene Bartlett, *These Are the Baptists* (Royal Oak, MI: Cathedral Publishers, 1972), 2.
2. Ibid.

2

Believer's Baptism
Questions That Need Answers

Bible Basis:
Acts 8:26–40

Objectives
At the end of the session youth will be able to:
- name three Baptist affirmations about baptism;
- connect a biblical story of baptism to each Baptist affirmation;
- answer in their own words at least three questions that may lead a person to baptism.

Key Bible Verse:
" 'What is to prevent me from being baptized?' " (Acts 8:36).

Background for the Leader

In a very real sense, baptism is what makes Baptists Baptist. At least it is the characteristic about us that people first noticed and by which we got our name. We baptize in a different way and at a different time than many other Christian groups do. We baptize people when they are old enough to understand what following Jesus Christ means and when they make such a commitment. When Baptists baptize, instead of sprinkling, they immerse the person in water.

As with our other beliefs, there is strong biblical support for the way Baptists baptize. The Greek word that in the New Testament is translated "baptize" means literally "to dip under." This form of baptism is grounded in the New Testament. The time of baptism is as well. Jesus was baptized as an adult. All the New Testament stories of baptism are of people who

were old enough to have experienced the saving grace of Jesus Christ in their lives, and they had made a conscious decision to accept Christ as their Lord and Savior.

We can clearly affirm a strong Baptist tradition regarding baptism. Baptism is for those who have experienced the saving power of Jesus Christ in their lives. Because their lives have been transformed by Christ, baptism is for those who are willing to commit to following in the way of Christ. This is what Baptists have affirmed since the day in 1609 when John Smyth baptized himself and a small band of believers in Holland and formed the first Baptist church.

Baptists believe in the baptism of believers. A person must be able to make a conscious decision that is based in his or her belief about Christ before asking to be baptized. Conscious commitment to Christ as Lord and Savior requires the asking and answering of important

6

questions related to life and faith. When the individuals affirm that the answers of the gospel are the answers that will shape their lives, they may be baptized. All of this assumes a maturity that enables an individual to make both decisions and commitments.

Baptists affirm baptism as a human response to God's action. God has acted in Jesus Christ to save us. That action is an invitation to us—an invitation to faith in God, who with great love, makes the sacrifice that brings salvation to us. Baptism is our response to that invitation. God offers us forgiveness of sins; baptism is the sign that we have accepted that offer. God gives the gift of new life in Jesus Christ; baptism is the sign that we have accepted that gift. God calls us to live lives worthy of the gift we have been given; baptism is the sign that we have accepted that call.

Baptists practice baptism by immersion. The literal meaning of baptize, "to dip under" or "to submerge," coupled with strong biblical support, upholds the Baptist practice of immersion. Baptism by immersion symbolizes the dying to the old life and rising again to new life in Christ. This reflects the experience of those who seek baptism and further supports the practice of immersion.

Exploring the Biblical Basis

The eunuch was an official in the Ethiopian court in charge of the queen's finances. In the heat of the day, he traveled a wilderness road on his way home. He was a religious man, or at the very least, a man with religious sensitivity. He had been in Jerusalem for worship, seeking to experience God more fully in his life. He was possibly a convert to Judaism or a God-fearer, someone who read the Law and participated in religious ceremonies but had not been circumcised and become a Jew. As he read the Scripture, he may have asked: How does this religion fit together? What difference will it make for my life? Is this something I can commit to without hesitation?

In this story, the eunuch is trying to understand just a bit more about faith. He seeks answers for himself and his life. Perhaps that would have been all, but God intervened. An angel of the Lord appeared to Philip and commanded him to go to this road, to meet this Ethiopian, to answer his questions, to lead him further along in his journey of faith, and to baptize him in the name of Jesus Christ.

This story comes at an interesting point in the Book of Acts. Persecution in Jerusalem caused believers to escape to the countryside. Philip went to Samaria. There he shared the Good News and baptized the Samaritans who came to believe in Jesus Christ. The story of the traveling Ethiopian immediately follows this story. In chapter 10, the story of the baptism of a Gentile named Cornelius is told. In bold fashion Acts tells the story of the spread of the gospel to increasingly different people. It describes the power of the gospel to touch and transform people in unexpected ways.

Baptism is the central focus of all of these people's experiences. Their baptism confirms their faith in Jesus Christ and publicly declares their commitment to the new life they have chosen to follow. From the earliest days of the church, baptism has played and continues to play that role in the lives of believers.

As you prepare for this lesson:

Pray for each youth by name. This session will have the most meaning for your students if it is directly related to their individual needs and interests. As you prepare, keep them in your prayers, remembering them, their lives, and their needs. Ask for God's presence with them during the week and when you gather for this session. Be particularly attentive to those who may not yet be baptized. Be open to ways you might encourage them to take this important step of faith.

Read and reflect on the Bible passage. Read the account of the Ethiopian's baptism in Acts 8:26–40. As you do so, place yourself in the role of the Ethiopian. Imagine the questions and concerns that he had as he contemplated the meaning of faith for his life. Then place yourself in the role of Philip. Consider the ways he might have responded to your young people. Then consider how you can most effectively respond to the youths' questions about faith and the meaning of baptism.

Beginning

1. **Baptism is . . .** (5–10 minutes)
   * Tell the youth that they will explore what Baptists believe about baptism.
   * Write the words "Baptism is . . ." on a sheet of newsprint or chalkboard.
   * Ask the class to brainstorm what they know about baptism (what it means, what happens when someone is baptized, what difference it makes for a person's life, etc.) by completing the sentence. Record their responses on the newsprint or chalkboard.
   * Quickly review the list, affirming their efforts.
   * Say: "This is a good beginning. Let's look at some basic Baptist beliefs about baptism."

2. **Three Baptist affirmations.** (5–10 minutes)
   * Distribute handout #2.
   * Ask a volunteer to read each of the three affirmations.
   * Illustrate each affirmation highlighting your church's practice.
   * Ask the youth to name at least three ways these Baptist beliefs are different from the beliefs and practices of other Christian churches. *(Key differences are: [1] Some other churches baptize infants. [2] Other churches believe baptism is more a means or a sign of God acting in the life of a person than the person's response to God's action. [3] Other ways of baptizing include sprinkling or pouring water on the person being baptized.)*

Exploring

3. **Bible reflection.** (15 minutes)
   * Ask youth to open their Bibles to Acts 8: 26–40.
   * Explain that this incident took place early in the history of the church when the sharing of the gospel was beginning to spread beyond the first early group of believers in Jerusalem.
   * Read the passage together.
   * Ask: "In what ways do the three Baptist affirmations about baptism appear in this story?"
   (To help you guide the discussion of each affirmation: 1. Baptists believe in the baptism of believers. The Ethiopian models a willingness to search, question, and understand the Scriptures. Just as the Ethiopian made a conscious decision based on his belief about Christ and then asked to be baptized, we affirm that all who seek baptism must be able to do the same. 2. Baptists affirm baptism as a human response to God's action. Philip explained to the Ethiopian that God acted through Jesus Christ to save us. The eunuch's decision to be baptized is a response to that. 3. Baptists practice baptism by immersion. This passage does not provide the details of the form of baptism used by Philip, but the indications are there for us. They "went down into the water, and Philip baptized him. . . . they came up out of the water.")

4. **A story from Baptist history.** (5 minutes)
   * Tell the class you are going to move 1,600 years through history to discover how these biblical ideas about baptism appeared in the life of the first Baptist church.
   * Read the story of John Smyth.
   * Point out how the Baptist view of baptism played a crucial role in the beginnings of the first Baptist church.

5. **Being Philip and the Ethiopian.**
   (15–20 minutes)
   - Say: "The story of the Ethiopian offers us much more than insight into our practice of baptism. It helps us understand what enables a person to make the commitment to Christ that leads to baptism. The Ethiopian's baptism happened because he asked questions about the meaning of Scripture. Philip was there, not only to provide answers, but to tell him more about 'the good news about Jesus.'"
   - Divide the class into two groups.
   - Explain to one group that you would like them to imagine that they are the Ethiopian. Ask them to list on newsprint the questions they think the Ethiopian would have asked before deciding to be baptized.
   - Explain to the other group that they are to imagine that they are Philip. Ask them to list on newsprint the things Philip would have wanted to share with the Ethiopian to help him make the decision to be baptized.
   - Let both groups know that what you just asked of them is on their handout and that they are welcome to use their Bibles as needed.
   - Explain that the Ethiopian group will get to ask the Philip group one of their questions and the Philip group will get to use their answers to respond. Tell them how much time they have to work and instruct them to begin.
   - Bring the class back together. Ask the Ethiopian group to ask the Philip group one of their questions. Ask the Philip group to share their answer. If they do not have one, ask the class to develop one. Continue to do this until all the questions have been asked or time is up. Then ask the Philip group to share any additional information they might have.

6. **Personalize Ethiopian/Philip roles.**
   (5–10 minutes)
   - Use the following questions, or questions of your own, to generate a discussion: For those of you who were "Philips":
     1. How did you (Philip) respond to God? How was it easy? Hard?
     2. What thoughts/feelings did you experience while teaching the Ethiopian and later baptizing him? (Give the class permission to make up answers to this question.)

   For those of you who were the "Ethiopian":
     1. How did you (the Ethiopian) respond to God? How was it easy? Hard?
     2. What did you do on you own that led to your baptism?
     3. What led you to ask to be baptized? (Give the class permission to make up answers to this question.)

Responding

7. **Exploring ways to be like the Ethiopian and/or Philip.** (5–10 minutes)
   - Say: "You might be asking questions about God and Christ. In time, your faith will lead you to deeper commitment to Christ, perhaps to baptism. Even if you have been baptized, you may still be asking questions. That is okay too. I'm here, as is the pastor, your parents perhaps, and other people in the church, to share 'the good news of Jesus' with you. If you already know Jesus, won't you help others to understand the gospel more fully too?"
   - Ask the youth to choose one of these roles to practice for the next week.
   - Invite all class members, whether or not they have been baptized, to ask the questions they need answers to in order to commit to Christ as Lord and Savior.
   - Encourage the group, even the ones who

are seeking, to share what they believe with an adult, a parent, a friend, or even themselves during the coming week.

- Invite the class to close with a prayer. Thank God for the questions and answers that lead us to deeper faith. Ask God to help each person deepen his or her commitment to Christ.

3

The Bible
Read a Good Book Lately?

Bible Basis:
2 Timothy 3:14–17

Objectives
At the end of the session, youth will be able to:
- tell in their own words about John Smyth's contribution to Baptist identity;
- list at least three reasons it is important to be faithful to God's Word.

Key Bible Verse:
"All Scripture is inspired by God and is useful for teaching the truth, rebuking error, correcting faults, and giving instruction for right living" (2 Timothy 3:16, TEV).

Background for the Leader

The teen years are a time of searching, of claiming one's own identity, of making crucial lifestyle choices. This can be a confusing, frustrating, even frightening time. Where can young people turn for help? Baptists believe that the Bible is a source of guidance, encouragement, support, and inspiration for people of all ages. The Bible is relevant to young people today. Biblical characters, like today's teenagers, struggled with their identity and beliefs and with their sense of purpose. The Bible provides a safe stepping stone for youth as they move toward adulthood.

The difficulty of navigating through the teen years has been well documented. Mixed messages abound: It's a time for partying, dude, but don't forget to work hard in school. Drugs and alcohol are cool, but it's important to stay fit. I need you, Mom and Dad, but, hey, just

leave me alone, okay? And sex? Just do it, but oh yeah, there's this thing about AIDS and unwanted pregnancies and Christian values.

Where can young people turn for help? Parents, friends, and teachers provide important insights, but for the Christian young person there is more. As followers of Christ, teens—as well as adults—are called by God to look to the Bible as a daily source of guidance, encouragement, support, and inspiration.

The Bible's relevance to young people today lies in understanding that the people in the Bible were similar to people of today. No one listened to rap centuries ago, and no one chose a certain brand of footwear as a fashion statement. But biblical characters were much like us in that they struggled with their own identity and beliefs and with their own sense of purpose in the world. The message to all people from a loving and caring God was the same then as today: You cannot make it on your own; you need to depend on God and be faithful to God's Word if you want to live a fulfilling—and eternal—life.

The Bible is above all a book of faith, a collective account of people who amid their daily lives and struggles were able to experience the living God. As we teach young people about the Bible, we teach the truth, rebuke error, correct faults, and give guidelines for right living. That's powerful stuff, and with God's help it will provide a safe stepping stone for youth as they move toward adulthood.

Exploring the Biblical Basis

The apostle Paul was facing his most trying hour. He sat alone in a Roman dungeon, convicted of a crime he had not committed, waiting to be executed. Most of his friends had left him alone to suffer. The work to which he had given his life was being overcome by persecution and defections. In spite of these afflictions, Paul showed no regret for the choices he had made. He remained faithful to Christ, fully confident that his death would lead him back to his Savior.

This is the context for Paul's second letter to Timothy. Paul's work as a missionary is over, and his life is coming to an end. It is doubtful that he will see Timothy again—and he may not have another chance to write. So in four stirring chapters he offers urgent advice as a veteran missionary to a younger colleague and friend. The message: Carry on. Keep the faith. Be a steadfast soldier for Christ even if that means personal suffering and persecution.

Paul also encourages Timothy to maintain his trust in God's Word. The Scriptures, Paul believes, are the sole antidote to a timid faith and corruption within the church. Paul had seen how leaders of his day had cast God's Word aside, dismissing it as a patchwork of Hebrew thought. He knew that "all scripture is inspired by God" (3:16) and that God's Word is "able to instruct you for salvation through faith in Christ Jesus" (3:15). These were powerful words written in the first century—words that are just as timely today for those who follow Christ.

As you prepare for this lesson:

Pray for each youth by name. Ask that God will use you this week to plant a seed in their lives. Ask God to help you nurture the seeds that are within them as well as a deep appreciation of and commitment to God's Word.

Read and reflect on the Bible passage. Think about how you can you help your students discover the importance of the Bible in their lives this week and in the weeks that follow, and ask God to make it so.

Special Materials

Craft materials for collage:

- newsprint
- construction paper
- scissors
- tape or glue
- colored markers
- magazines and newspapers

Beginning

1. **Take a "Basketball Bible Quiz."** (5–10 minutes)
   - Form two teams by dividing the class.
   - Instruct the youth about the process: You will ask each team questions. Correct answers will score the number of points indicated on the question.
   - Ask the following questions. *(If you have a class that is overly competitive, you may want to eliminate the use of teams and simply ask the questions to the entire class.)*
     1. How many books are in the Bible? *(66; 2 pts.)*
     2. Name the two original languages of the Bible. *(Hebrew, Greek; 3 pts.)*

3. Where did Adam and Eve meet? *(Garden of Eden; 2 pts.)*

4. What is the second book of the Bible? *(Exodus; 2 pts.)*

5. Why did Moses flee Pharaoh for the land of Midian? *(Moses had killed an Egyptian; 2 pts.)*

6. On what mountain did Moses receive the Ten Commandments from God? *(Mount Sinai; 2 pts.)*

7. Who was the female prophet used by God to free the Israelites from King Jabin? *(Deborah; 3 pts.)*

8. Who is considered the greatest of the writing prophets? *(Isaiah; 3 pts.)*

9. Name the four Gospels. *(Matthew, Mark, Luke, John; 2 pts.)*

10. Who were the political and religious leaders of Jesus' time? *(Pharisees, Sadducees; 3 pts.)*

11. Where did Jesus begin his ministry? *(Galilee; 2 pts.)*

12. Who were the first two disciples called by Jesus? *(Simon, Andrew; 3 pts.)*

13. Who started to sink when he tried walking on the water to get to Jesus? *(Peter; 2 pts.)*

14. Where was Saul headed when he was struck down by God and converted? *(Damascus; 2 pts.)*

15. Who wrote the Letter to the Romans? *(Paul; 2 pts.)*

Bonus Points

Instruct the two teams to work separately to compile a list of the books known as letters attributed to Paul in the Bible. Each team will score one point for each book named. *(Romans; 1 Corinthians; 2 Corinthians; Galatians; Ephesians; Philippians; Colossians; 1 Thessalonians; 2 Thessalonians; 1 Timothy; 2 Timothy; Titus; Philemon).*

- Congratulate the youth on their efforts.

2. **Read about John Smyth.** (10 minutes)
   - Distribute handout #3.
   - Ask the youth to turn to "Meet John Smyth" on the handout.
   - Preface the story by emphasizing the theme for this session. Explain that our love for and obedience to the Scriptures date back to the earliest Baptists in England. The contributions of John Smyth and others gave Baptists a reputation as being a "people of the Book."
   - Invite volunteers to read aloud about John Smyth as others follow along.
   - Ask the class to complete this sentence on the handout: I think John Smyth's contributions to Baptist life are important today because . . .
   - Invite volunteers to share their responses with the rest of the class.

Exploring

3. **Make a collage based on 2 Timothy 3:14–17.** (15 minutes)
   - Ask the youth to turn in their Bibles to 2 Timothy 3:14–17.
   - Before having students read this text aloud, provide appropriate background from "Exploring the Biblical Basis."
   - Ask a volunteer to read the Scripture.
   - Repeat the key verse: 2 Timothy 3:16.
   - Ask these or your own questions:
     1. What do you think the phrase "inspired by God" means?
     2. What truths does the Bible teach?
     3. What faults does the Bible correct?
     4. In what ways does the Bible help us to live "right lives"?
   - Inform the youth that they are to work together to make a collage that illustrates their interpretation of verse 16. *(They can use words, drawings, symbols, magazine photos, newspaper stories, and so forth to create the collage. Provide help as needed, especially in getting the class started.)*

- When the collage is completed, ask the youth to talk about why they made the choices they did.

4. **Make personal Bible crests.** (10 minutes)
   - Explain that a family crest in medieval times was often a personal statement about things that were important to a particular family. Since the Bible is important to Baptists—as a large denominational family and as individual persons—it is appropriate to make Bible crests that indicate what is important to each of us about the Bible. *(Instructions for the crest can be found on the handout. You may want to distribute sheets of construction paper to the students so that they can make a larger, more colorful crest.)*
   - Reviewing the directions.
   - After about 10 minutes bring the group together.
   - Invite the youth to share their work.

Responding

5. **Write a letter.** (5–10 minutes)
   - In your own words say: "Paul loved to write letters to his friends and colleagues. His writing was so faith-filled and beautiful that many of his letters are part of the New Testament. In Paul's second letter to Timothy, he urged his friend to remain obedient to God and faithful to God's Word."
   - Ask each youth to think of one person—a family member, friend, or neighbor—with whom they would like to share God's message in the Bible or whom they would like to encourage to read the Bible more often. They may even write a letter to themselves.
   - Instruct them to write a letter to that person—just as Paul wrote to Timothy—encouraging her or him to be faithful to God's Word. Let the youth know that their letters will not be shared with the class, so they may be personal and persuasive, perhaps providing their own testimony about how the Bible has helped them.
   - When they are finished writing, suggest that they take time to reread their letter, imagining that they have just received it in the mail from a friend.
   - Ask: "What effect would the letter have on them?"
   - Suggest that the youth consider mailing their letters if they are comfortable doing so.

6. **Close in song and prayer.** (5 minutes)
   - Close with one of the group's favorite celebration songs. One possibility is "Whose Side Are You Leaning On?"
   - Close in a circle prayer.
   - Give thanks for God's Word and for your time together today.

4

Priesthood of All Believers
But God, I'm Just a Teenager

Bible Basis:
Revelation 1:4–6

Objectives
At the end of the session youth will be able to:

- describe "priesthood of all believers";
- explain two ways in which they function as priests.

Key Bible Verse:
"[Christ] loves us and freed us from our sins by his blood, and made us to be a kingdom, priests serving his God and Father" (Revelation 1:5–6).

Background for the Leader

The "priesthood of all believers" is one of the foundational Baptist principles. Such important emphases as religious liberty and ministry of the laity are based in it. Our understanding of church governance and discipleship grow out of it. It would be difficult to name any principle that is more basic to Baptist life and thought.

But what is the priesthood of all believers? Quite simply it is the conviction that "every Christian is a priest before God and to the world."[1] Being a priest before God means that each one of us stands directly before God with no need for intermediaries. No one tells us what we must believe about God or how we must relate to God. Each of us receives the blessings of salvation and grace directly from God, and each of us is accountable directly to God for our life and faith. Being a priest to the world means that each of us is called by God to

a ministry within the world. We are God's representatives, God's agents. As such, we bring God's love to the world.

The priesthood of all believers has particular reference to the relationship between laity and clergy in a Baptist church. It prescribes an equality before God characterized by a shared ministry between laity and ordained clergy. If there is a differentiation between laity and clergy, it is one of *role,* not importance, power, or prestige. When a church ordains a person, it is, in this sense, saying, "We see you are gifted to play a role of leadership within the church. This will be your ministry." In this manner, ordained clergy are not essentially different from the laity; they are just set apart to use particular gifts.

In the same way, the priesthood of *all* believers maintains that youth are not essentially different from adults. All are free to stand before God to receive the gift of salvation. All who follow Christ are responsible for ministering in

Christ's name—in their schools, in their homes, within the community, and beyond.

It's easy for many youth to dismiss the notion that they are priests and are therefore responsible for their relationship with God and for their role in the church's ministry. Like Moses or Jeremiah in the Old Testament, they may think they are not skilled enough or experienced enough. Like many would-be followers of Jesus in the New Testament, they may still have a "hand to the plow," caught up in the busyness of their lives.

This old Baptist concept of the priesthood of all believers has particular relevance for youth today. To know that they are God's very own—both to receive God's blessings and to take up God's ministry—can be a tremendously affirming thought to young people as they struggle with issues of identity and self-worth. Junior and senior high youth are important to God and critical to the work of Christ's church!

With this status comes a responsibility to reflect God's love to other people, to be a priest for others. Youth and adults alike are called to serve God by serving others. They can be "ministers" for God among their friends, family, and neighbors in real and practical ways. Youth have opportunities to reflect the gospel message in settings where adults cannot be as effective. This is both their privilege and responsibility as followers of Christ.

Exploring the Biblical Basis

The Book of Revelation is one of the most difficult Bible books to understand because it is written in a style called apocalyptic writing, which is unfamiliar to many of us. It is difficult to grasp the book's full meaning with great certainty, yet at points it speaks directly and clearly to us about our lives as Christians. The passage that is the biblical basis for this session is such a point.

Revelation is written as a letter. Our passage comes from the introduction of the letter, which gives the sender's name, the addressees,

and a greeting. The letter is from John to the seven churches in Asia. The greeting offers grace and peace in the name of Jesus Christ. As part of the greeting John reminds his readers of what Jesus Christ did for all who believe. Christ loves us and freed us from our sins by his sacrificial death. Building upon the Old Testament concept of the priesthood but expanding it to include all believers, John then states that Christ made us a kingdom of priests. Here we have one of several direct New Testament references to the priesthood of all believers. (The others are found in 1 Peter 2:5, 9 and Revelation 5:9–10; 20:6). William Barclay describes it this way: "[John] means that because of what Jesus Christ did, access to the presence of God is not now confined to priests in the narrowest sense of the term, but that it is open to every [person]. Every[one] is a priest. There is a priesthood of all believers. We can come boldly unto the throne of grace (Hebrews 4:16), because for us there is a new and living way into the presence of God."[2] The passage goes on to say that service is a part of our priesthood—serving God, doing the work of God, being involved in ministry.

When these two understandings of priesthood, access and service, are held together, we begin to capture a sense of what the priesthood of all believers is about. John made a grand claim. Israel was quite comfortable with the notion that access and service, priesthood, was appropriate for a select few. To say, however, that it was for *all* believers was a radically new understanding. That radically new understanding of priesthood remains central to the life and thought of Baptists.

As you prepare for this lesson:

Pray for each youth by name. Ask that God will use this session to speak to each one's heart. Ask that, through you, they might sense the wonder of personal and direct access to God. Pray that the fulfillment that comes from service to God in the ministry of Christ's church may be made real.

Read and reflect on the Bible passage. Think about ways in which you have experienced a personal and direct relationship with God in your own life. Consider ways in which you believe you have been chosen by God to minister to others. What is special about this passage that you would like to pass on?

Beginning

1. **Introduce the theme.** (5 minutes)
   • Write on newsprint or a chalkboard: "A minister is . . ."
   • Invite the youth to complete this sentence popcorn style.
   • After several responses add: "A priest is . . ."
   • Invite the youth to complete this sentence popcorn style.
   • Facilitate a brief discussion using these or your own questions:
     1. What are the similarities and differences between a minister and a priest?
     2. What are the requirements for being a minister or priest?
     3. How are the roles of ministers and priests in various churches similar and different?
     4. What kinds of people are ministers and priests?
     5. Whom do you know who is a minister or priest?
   • Use these or your own words to introduce the priesthood of all believers: Although Baptists don't use the word *priest* to refer to a particular person in the church, we still believe in the importance of priests. In fact, it is one of the most important of all Baptist beliefs. What we believe is called "the priesthood of all believers." That means we believe that everyone who believes in Christ and is a member of a church is a priest—everyone! It also means that we believe that everyone is a minister

too! In this session we'll be exploring what it means to be a priest and how we are and can be priests.

Exploring

2. **Read the Bible passage.** (5–10 minutes)
   • Ask youth to turn to Revelation 1:4–6 in their Bibles.
   • Use the material in "Exploring the Biblical Basis" to introduce the passage. Note these points particularly:
     • The book of Revelation is written in the form of a letter.
     • This passage is from the introduction to the letter.
     • In it the writer, John, greets his readers and reminds them of what Christ has done for them.
   • Ask youth to listen for the things John says that Christ has done for them as the passage is read.
   • Read the Bible passage.
   • Ask youth to share what they heard.
   • List their responses on the chalkboard or newsprint. *(Responses should include: Christ loves us, freed us from our sin, made us a kingdom of priests.)*
3. **Explore "What's So Special about a Priest?"** (10–15 minutes)
   • Distribute handout #4.
   • Ask youth to look at the section "What's So Special about a Priest?"
   • Read the first paragraph.
   • Use information from "Background for the Leader" to expand on what you read.
   • Guide a discussion on the two special roles of priests to help youth understand ways in which they can act as priests. Include these points:
     • Direct access to God is experienced in our own personal relationship with God. We can ask for forgiveness directly. We can receive God's forgiveness directly. We can hear

God's call to us directly. We can develop our own understanding of how God is at work in our lives. Our direct access to God is also for others. We can go directly to God to pray for others and their needs.

- The ministry we have from God is the role we play in doing God's work in the world. That can be as basic as sharing God's love by being loving ourselves. It can include evangelism as we talk about God with others. It can include social action as we are involved in activities that make God's love and justice real in the world. All of this can happen in all areas of our lives: at home, at school, at work, with our friends, in our communities, anywhere we are.

4. **Play "People Bingo."** (10 minutes)
   - Refer to the "People Bingo" card on the handout.
   - Ask a youth to read aloud the opening paragraph.
   - Review the directions for the activity, emphasizing that the youth should try to get everyone in the class to sign at least one square.
   - Allow several minutes for the youth to mingle among one another to complete the activity.
   - Invite those who got a "Bingo" to read the person's name and the way they acted as a priest as indicated in the box.
   - Give thanks for the many ways in which youth are already serving as priests.

5. **Assess readiness to be a priest.** (5–10 minutes)
   - Ask the youth to look at the section "Are You Up to the Task?" on the handout.
   - Review the directions for this activity. Encourage the class to respond honestly to each statement—there is no right or wrong answer.

- When the students are done, designate three sections of the room "agree," "disagree," and "undecided."
- Tell the class that you are going to read a statement. They are to move to the section of the room that corresponds with the answer they circled.
- Read all or selected statements one at a time. Allow time for youth to move. After each, facilitate a brief discussion by asking: "Why are you standing where you are?"
- Ask youth to return to their seats.
- Ask them to silently reflect on the "Questions for Reflection" on the handout and to write their answers.
- Lead the class in a discussion of their responses to the questions.

Responding

6. **Identify ways to be a priest.** (5 minutes)
   - Ask youth to turn to "Ready to Be a Priest" on the handout.
   - Read the instructions.
   - Allow time for individual work to complete the section.
   - Invite those who are willing to share what they have written.

7. **Close with prayer.** (5 minutes)
   - Close with a circle prayer.
   - Invite each youth to thank God in his or her own way, silently or aloud.
   - Affirm that we are all part of a royal priesthood of believers.
   - Encourage youth to be faithful to their role as priests during the coming week.

Notes

1. Walter B. Shurden, ed., *Proclaiming the Baptist Vision: The Priesthood of All Believers* (Macon, GA: Smyth and Helwys, 1993), 2.
2. William Barclay, *The Revelation of John* (Philadelphia: Westminster Press, 1959), 1:44.

5

Religious Liberty
Free—Even in School!

Bible Basis:
Acts 5:17–32

Objectives
At the end of the session youth will be able to:

- give a biblical reason for religious freedom;
- explain why Baptists oppose mandated prayer in public school;
- describe religious activities that are appropriate in the public school setting.

Key Bible Verse:
"'We must obey God rather than any human authority'" (Acts 5:29).

Background for the Leader

They are two of our greatest legacies—the theological principle of religious liberty and the constitutional doctrine of separation of church and state. Because of Baptists, they are part of America's fabric of life. From early colonial days Baptists have worked to establish and maintain religious freedom.

Maintaining a consistent Baptist witness for freedom hasn't always been easy. Our Baptist forebears were whipped and imprisoned. Even today many advocates of this Baptist emphasis are criticized and ridiculed. When Baptists speak of religious liberty, they mean that decisions about faith and one's relationship with God are up to the individual, not the state. Baptists believe that the church can maintain its purpose and integrity best if it exists free from government interference whether supportive or hostile. In this session we will look at a biblical passage in which the early church

and its leaders deal with this issue of outside interference. We will also explore some of the important reasons religious freedom continues to be an important concern for us as Baptists.

Early Baptists didn't see things in the usual and customary way. They had different notions than most people about what it meant to be faithful and how to respond to Christ's claims on their lives. They often got into trouble with the authorities, and these experiences shaped the Baptist understanding of religious freedom. By the grace of God, Baptists forged the experiences of religious persecution into an understanding of religious freedom. Previously, religious persecution had led to the establishment of a new authority that imposed its will on others. Baptists sought to provide freedom for all religious beliefs and expressions.

Baptists have been present whenever religious freedom has been talked about. Roger Williams, although a Baptist for only a few months, was instrumental in establishing Rhode

Island as a place of religious freedom and in making Baptists acutely aware of the need for this freedom. Isaac Backus, a Massachusetts Baptist pastor, was a tireless proponent of this same freedom before the Continental Congress in the eighteenth century. John Leland, a Virginia Baptist pastor, played a vitally important role in the effort to secure a Bill of Rights that guaranteed religious freedom. Baptists have also been present whenever religious freedom has been threatened.

Presidents Jefferson and Madison supported the secular rationale for separation of church and state. This view maintains a "high wall of separation"; it prohibits government action from imposing religion in people's lives.

A second rationale for religious freedom is evangelical in its approach. This view is based in our historic Baptist principle of soul freedom. Soul freedom is the right and responsibility of the individual to stand before God and make decisions regarding his or her relationship with God. In this view, the purpose of separation of church and state is not to protect persons *from* religion but to protect them *for* religion. Its purpose is to enable the unfettered development of faith. It seeks to protect both the individual Christian and the church from interference from the state that can thwart vital and vibrant faith.

The secular view of separation, for example, objects to state-mandated prayer out of a concern that prayer not be imposed on those who don't believe in it. The evangelical view of separation objects to state-mandated prayer because it believes firmly in the value, meaning, and power of prayer and refuses to let the state determine what prayer is and when it should happen.

The Baptist view of the need for separation of church and state has placed us in the company of those who have a much more secular view of life than we do. It has opened us to attacks that we are not truly "religious" or that we do not care about faith. But Baptists take faith very seriously. Baptists are suspicious of

any apart from the church who would attempt to define what religion is and tell us how to practice it.

Exploring the Biblical Basis

Peter and John had been in trouble before. Acts 3:1–4:31 tells the story of their arrest for preaching about Christ in the temple and healing a crippled beggar. After spending a night in jail, the two were brought before the council. Facing his accusers, Peter gave an impassioned speech that outlined basic Christian teaching about Christ and his resurrection. He claimed that it was this power that enabled them to heal the crippled man. Amazed at their boldness but fearful their message would spread, the authorities ordered them to never preach or heal in Jesus' name again. Peter and John replied, "Whether it is right in God's sight to listen to you rather than to God, you must judge; for we cannot keep from speaking about what we have seen and heard" (Acts 4:19–20). They then went home and prayed for boldness. Their prayer was answered, and the apostles returned to the temple to heal and preach.

It wasn't long before the apostles were back in jail. That story is in Acts 5:17–32. This time an angel appeared during the night to set them free. Back to the temple they went. The next morning the council assembled and commanded that the apostles be brought before them. Instead, one of the temple police reported that, even though all the doors were still locked, the prisoners were nowhere to be found. Everyone was stunned. Then more shocking news followed: the men they had jailed were preaching in the temple. Once again the apostles were brought before the council, which demanded that they explain the defiance of their orders. Peter said simply, "We must obey God rather than any human authority" (Acts 5:29).

A number of stories in Acts portray the early church establishing its identity, both as a fellowship of believers and in relationship with the outside world. A feature of these stories is the issue of authority: In what will we trust? Whom will we follow? This passage clearly affirms that no one or nothing except God will determine who we are or what we do. This stance led directly to the persecution suffered by the early church. It set Christians in direct conflict with religious and political authorities who sought to determine what others should think and do, what they should believe, and how they should worship. Written following the early days of persecution, this passage reflects a central tenet of the church's identity. It affirms the historical reality and the contemporary challenge that to be the church, to be persons and communities of faith, is to owe ultimate allegiance to God.

As you prepare for this lesson:

Pray for each of the youth by name. Teaching is more than an intellectual exercise. It is an opportunity to enter into the lives of the youth in a way that will enable them to grow in faith and relationship with God. Pray that God will help you do that. As you read this material and prepare for class, keep each of the class members in prayer. Pray for an understanding of the session that will enable youth to make their faith a more vital part of their school experience.

Read and reflect on the Bible passage. Read the account of Peter before the council. Be especially attentive to the radical nature of his statement, "We must obey God rather than any human authority." To grasp the impact of what he said, it might be helpful to imagine someone saying the same thing in a courtroom or at a congressional hearing today. How would those in authority respond? This will be a discussion question in class, so it will be helpful if you have thought about it. Also consider the meaning of such a statement for us today. Is the need to speak and live with the boldness Peter showed less for us because we live in a nation that allows religious freedom?

Acts 3:1–4:31 provides important background information on this passage. It will be helpful for you to read this in order to understand the events that led up to the incident described in Acts 5.

Beginning

1. **Statements about religion and school.** (5–10 minutes)
   - Give a brief overview of the class by saying that you will be talking about school and religion.
   - Distribute handout #5.
   - Ask the youth to answer the true or false questions listed under "Religion and School—Dos and Don'ts" on their handout. *(For your information, but not to share with the youth at this point, all the answers are true.)*
   - Give the youth a few moments to complete the "quiz" on their own or complete it together.
   - Ask the youth to share their responses.
   - Encourage brief discussions following each question by asking them to share the reasons for their answers.
   - Refrain from telling them the correct responses. Let them know that they will explore the correct answers later in the class.

Exploring

2. **Bible reflection.** (5 minutes)
   - In your own words and using "Background for the Leader," make these points:
     - Prayer and other religious expressions in schools are important concerns related to the principle of separation of church and state.
     - Baptists were instrumental in the adoption of the Bill of Rights, which provides a guarantee of religious freedom to Americans.
     - The Bible supports Baptists' belief regarding the separation of church

and state, including the passage you will look at now.

- Ask students to turn to Acts 5:17–32.
- Use "Exploring the Biblical Basis" to set the scene.
- Ask for volunteer(s) to read the Scripture.
- Guide a brief discussion using the following questions:
  1. Who are the "authorities" in your life?
  2. In what ways do you obey them?
  3. Why did Peter insist that he should not obey "human authority"?
  4. What are some situations in the world today in which it is necessary for you, as a Christian, to obey God rather than human authority?
  5. What are some situations in school today in which it is necessary for you, as a Christian, to obey God rather than human authority?

3. **Baptist views of separation of church and state.** (5 minutes)
- Ask the youth to read the affirmation of separation of church and state on their handout:
  "Baptists believe that in order for faith to be meaningful it must be free. Separation of church and state is needed so that people can develop their faith and relationship with God free from interference from the government."
- Explain that this is the traditional view Baptists hold regarding the need for separation of church and state. Note that its purpose is not to limit faith; it is to ensure that there is freedom for faith to develop fully and deeply.
- Ask:
  1. In what way(s) does Peter's statement, about obeying God rather than human authority, support this view of the separation of church and state? *(It removes the state from matters of faith so that God can be obeyed.)*

  2. What are some ways in which this same principle would apply to the issue of religious expression in public schools? *(The school acts as the government. It is the human authority that would not be obeyed if it became involved in matters of faith and religion.)*

4. **Religion and schools guidelines.** (10 minutes)
- Divide the class into small groups of three.
- Assign each group statements about "Religion in Public Schools" from their handout.
- Ask them to read each statement and, using observations or experiences from school, to illustrate how religion is or is not practiced in school.
- After 3–4 minutes, and before bringing the students together, ask them to find the questions on the True-False quiz they took earlier that correspond with their statements and to determine the correct answer.
- Bring the students back together and ask each group to share their work. As necessary ask:
  "Does our discussion support or challenge your illustration of the way schools and religion come together/remain separated? How?"

Responding

5. **Current law debate.** (15–20 minutes)
- Explain that people still disagree about these laws even though current law on these subjects can be determined.
- Facilitate a brief discussion using the following questions:
  1. With which policy(s) that you just researched do you disagree? Why?
  2. Should prayer be allowed in school? Why or why not?
  3. Should teachers be permitted to

participate in a religious club? Why or why not?

4. Should Christmas be celebrated because it is such a popular holiday? Why or why not?

5. Should the creation story in Genesis be taught as part of the science curriculum? Why or why not?

- Select one issue on which the youth disagree.
- Divide them randomly into two teams.
- Tell one team they are to support the current law; the other to oppose it.
- Tell the youth they have a few minutes to organize their thoughts to support their "view."
- Bring the two sides together and facilitate a debate.

6. **Decide on action.** (5 minutes)
- Ask the youth to complete one of these sentences, which you have written on the chalkboard or newsprint:

- One thing I can do about the practice of religion in my school that is not in accord with what we have learned is . . .
  (With whom can they talk? How should they raise the questions? How can they work for change?)
- One thing I can do, within the guidelines we just researched, to increase a religious presence in my school is . . .
  (What do the guidelines permit that is not being done? Are there some things students would like to begin?)
- Close with prayer. Thank God for Peter and for the early Baptists' bold witness, for their courage to obey God rather than any human authority. Ask God for a similar kind of boldness to live out our faith too.

6

Autonomy of the Local Church
It's Up to Us to Be the Church

Bible Basis:
Acts 2:40–47

Objectives
At the end of the session youth will be able to:

- describe two key elements of the Baptist principle "congregational autonomy";
- name at least three key elements of a church they would like to create.

Key Bible Verse:
"They devoted themselves to the apostles' teaching and fellowship, to the breaking of bread and the prayers" (Acts 2:42).

Background for the Leader

Baptists have a different understanding of the church than most people do. For us the local congregation is the key because it is representative of the whole church of Jesus Christ. It is free to govern its own affairs, to order its worship, to decide how and with what other churches it will relate. Baptists call this freedom "congregational autonomy." Yet Baptist churches are not just isolated congregations. From the earliest times we have seen the need to gather in associations to do things we cannot do alone and to seek counsel and advice from one another. At times these two realities have created tension among us as we have sought to balance them appropriately in the midst of sometimes contentious issues. The principles remain valid, however; and it is those principles that are the focus of this session.

Congregational autonomy is, in the words of William Keucher, former president of the

American Baptist Churches, "the right of each congregation (1) to choose its own ministers and officers, (2) to establish its own covenant membership and discipline and confessions, (3) to order its life in its own organizational forms with its constitution and bylaws, (4) to implement its right to belong to other denominational agencies and ecumenical church bodies, (5) to own and to control its own property and budget."[1] More recently historian Walter Shurden has affirmed several of these points and lifted up some new ones. He writes in his book *The Baptist Identity: Four Fragile Freedoms*, "Church freedom is the historic Baptist affirmation that local churches are free, under the Lordship of Jesus Christ, to determine their membership and leadership, to order their worship and work, to ordain whom they perceive as gifted for ministry, male or female, and to participate in the larger Body of Christ, of whose unity and mission Baptists are proudly a part."[2]

This means that every Baptist congregation

has the freedom to be the church it believes God has called it to be. And as is always the case, with the freedom comes a great responsibility—to listen and respond to God's call to be the church in a particular time and place.

First, let's deal with the freedom. The Baptist concept of the church is grounded in the concrete reality of the local congregation. That congregation is free to determine its corporate life and its relationships with others. We believe that it is this grounding that brings life to the church and enables it to faithfully respond to God's call to ministry both within its own walls and to the world. No predetermined hierarchical system dictates to congregations. There are no bishops, no outside controlling groups. Each congregation can set its standards for membership, determine its structure and organization, choose its style of worship. Certainly there is much in common among Baptist churches in these areas, but each congregation is free to change as it understands God's will for itself.

Included in this freedom is the freedom to relate to other churches through denominational and ecumenical structures. As part of these relationships, the structures may set additional criteria for membership and participation. At times there is significant debate over what those criteria should be. Once they are decided, however, each congregation retains its right to determine whether or not to continue in relationship with those structures. That freedom is a given, the very core of congregational autonomy.

With this freedom, however, comes the great responsibility of being the church—of listening for and responding to God's call so that the congregation will remain faithful in its life and ministry. No one can tell a local Baptist congregation what it must be and do except God. The congregation's responsibility is to listen and obey when God speaks. Thus, each local congregation needs to develop a listening stance, refusing to be so caught up in its own issues and survival that it cannot hear God's voice. It must constantly be open to change, willing to move in new directions when God calls and willing to risk seeing and doing things differently from others in obedience to God's will. Each congregation must bear its own responsibility rather than relying on bishops or outside structures to tell it how to be faithful.

Exploring the Biblical Basis

The Bible passage for this session is the first description of a church in the New Testament. Although only a few verses, it tells us much about the nature of the church and the life of a local congregation.

The story picks up immediately following the gift of the Holy Spirit at Pentecost. Peter has preached a great sermon proclaiming the Good News of Jesus Christ. Many believe. Those who do are gathered into a community of faith that is the church.

Key Baptist principles about the church are illustrated in this passage. *The church is a community of believers* (v. 41). Baptists call it "regenerate church membership." This means that only those who have experienced the saving and transforming power of Jesus Christ in their lives are ready for membership. *Baptism is the introductory rite of membership* (v. 41). Those who believed were baptized and became members of the church. This is one of several biblical reference points for our belief in believer's baptism. *Learning, fellowship, worship, and prayer are essential elements of congregational life* (vv. 42, 46–47). These words, while not all-inclusive, are the first that describe congregational life in the early church. They still inform us about the important elements of congregational life today. *Wondrous things happen within the fellowship of the church* (v. 43). The passage refers to them as "wonders and signs." They testify to a faith in the great things that happen when two or three are gathered together in the name of Christ. *There is a great intimacy of sharing within the congregation* (vv. 44–45). The passage speaks of everyone selling their possessions and holding everything in common. While most churches do not follow that practice today, it is an appropriate image for the depth of commitment to one another that is to be found within a congregation. *As powerful as this community experience is for those who share it, there is always an openness to others, a desire to incorporate new believers whom God provides* (vv. 41, 47). The power of the gospel and the love that is evident in the community attract others, and the congregation is always open to receive them.

From the New Testament perspective all of this happens within the context of the local congregation. There are no church structures and hierarchies. These words, which are used to describe the very first church, are words that shape the life and faith of local congregations.

As you prepare for this lesson:

Pray for each youth by name. Each member of your class attaches some meaning to church as it is made real for them in the local congregation. For some youth these meanings may be very positive; others may have decidedly mixed feelings about the church and your congregation. As you pray for the youth, focus on their experiences of church. Pray that through this session they may develop a clearer understanding of the freedom and responsibility of being the church together.

Read and reflect on the Bible passage. Use the material in "Exploring the Bible Basis" to guide your reflection on the passage. Consider ways in which you have experienced each of these principles in your own life and congregation. Reflect on the elements that are missing in your own life and how that might be changed. To get a full picture of the context of this passage, you may want to read the story of Pentecost, which begins in Acts 2:1.

Special Materials

Art supplies for step 3—such things as:
- markers
- chalk
- glue
- tape
- buttons
- glitter
- fabric
- Popsicle sticks
- silk flowers
- felt
- ribbon
- acorns
- pine cones
- twigs

Beginning

1. **Read and reflect on the Bible passage.** (5–10 minutes)
   - Welcome the youth.
   - Explain that in today's session you will be taking a look at the church, especially what Baptists think about the church.
   - Ask them to open their Bibles to Acts 2: 40–47.
   - Tell the youth that the Bible passage you will look at today is the first description of a church in the New Testament.
   - Briefly explain the events of Pentecost that are described in Acts 2:1–39.
   - Ask a volunteer to read Acts 2:40–47.

Exploring

2. **What is a church?** (5–10 minutes)
   - Distribute handout #6.
   - Ask the youth to turn to "What Is a Church?" on the handout.
   - Explain that each of the statements is based on the passage they just read.
   - Ask them to find the verse(s) in the passage that relate to each statement and to record their answers.
   - After they find the correct verse(s) for each statement ask: "In what ways do you see or do you not see that element present in our church? Do you think it should be there? Why or why not?" (*The material in "Exploring the Bible Background" will help you with this step.*)

3. **Create a church.** (20–25 minutes)
   - Say: "We'll be looking at Baptist beliefs about the church later in the session. For now it's important to know that one basic Baptist belief is that every local congregation is free to shape its own

life and ministry. That means we have the freedom to be the kind of church we believe God wants us to be. No one can tell us what we have to do. Right now I'd like us to take advantage of that freedom and pretend that we are starting all over to create a church. What would you like it to be like? What about our present church would you keep? What would you change?"

- Have a variety of art supplies available for youth to choose from.
- Divide the class into groups of three.
- Instruct each group to look at the "Create a Church" section in their handout.
- Ask the youth to write their suggestions about the kinds of things they would want if they could design a church.
- After 3–4 minutes ask each small group to actually create the church they would like to attend. Encourage them to think about what they like and don't like about their present church. What would they add? (You might suggest that they develop symbols for some elements of the church such as caring or love for one another.)
- After 10–15 minutes ask the youth to share the churches they created. Ask them to describe the qualities of the church as well as the building.
- After each group has shared their "church," ask: "Is it possible for us to create churches like these? Why or why not?"

4. **Consider the freedom and responsibility of the local congregation.** (5–10 minutes)
   - Ask the youth to turn to "What Baptists Think about the Church" on the handout.

- Remind them that thinking about the kind of church they would like to create wouldn't mean anything if they didn't have the freedom to do it.
- Read together the paragraphs in this section. *(Material in "Background for the Leader" will help you discuss this further.)*
- Ask: In what ways does our church and the churches you created incorporate these Baptist beliefs?

Responding

5. **Close with prayer.** (5 minutes)
   - Review the key elements the youth would like to include in the churches they create.
   - Remind them that because of our Baptist beliefs about the church they have both the freedom and the responsibility to help make those things happen.
   - Invite the youth to stand in a circle.
   - Ask each person to contribute to the closing prayer in the following way. The leader says the first word(s), "Dear God," then the person to his or her left adds one word or a phrase, such as "Thank you. . . ." The next person to the left adds a word or a phrase, "for . . . ," and so on until a sentence is constructed by the circle. When everyone has had a turn, the leader says, "Amen."

Notes

1. William H. Keucher, "Congregational Autonomy," *Baptist Leader*, March 1976, 49.
2. Walter Shurden, *The Baptist Identity: Four Fragile Freedoms* (Macon, GA: Smyth and Helwys, 1993), 33.

7

Ministry of the Laity
Someone's Calling

Bible Basis:
Ephesians 4:1–7,11–13

Objectives
At the end of the session youth will be able to:

- describe at least three ways God calls people to ministry;
- identify at least three ways they work for Christ;
- discuss a possible way in which God is calling them.

Key Bible Verse:
". . . for the work of ministry, for building up the body of Christ . . ." (Ephesians 4:12).

Background for the Leader

Ministry of the laity is part of our Baptist tradition. Yet some people believe that one of the greatest challenges facing the church today is the need to rework the relationship between clergy and laity. This view is forcefully presented by church consultant Loren Mead in his book *Five Challenges for the Once and Future Church*.[1] Mead argues that an important part of meeting that challenge will be the development of a better understanding of the role of the laity as those who have a ministry both within the church and in the world. Our purpose in this session is to explore the ministry of the laity—its tradition and its biblical foundation— and understand more fully what it means for us. As we do this, we'll discover that this important principle impacts a great variety of issues that have to do with church governance and leadership. It has great implications for the appropriate role of clergy, influences the way we approach pastoral care within the congregation, and shapes our understanding of who does mission work and how it is done. As you look at this issue, focus on God's call as it comes to each disciple and its impact in shaping each person's ministry.

The phrase "ministry of the laity" conjures up a wide variety of images in people's minds. One view suggests that laity can and should play an active part in the church's ministry by serving on boards and committees, making budget decisions, and leading in worship. The focus of ministry is inside. It can include jobs some churches hire paid staff to do but which others leave to the laity.

A more expansive and more biblically appropriate understanding of ministry of the laity begins with the recognition that *all* disciples of Jesus Christ have a ministry to which they are called. For some that ministry is inside the church; for many more it is outside. The ministries to which laity are called are both within the church and in the world.

Ministry of the laity affirms the importance of participation of the laity in what are often seen as clergy responsibilities. They share in pastoral care as well as in leadership in worship. They preside at the Lord's Table, offering prayers of thanks and blessing for the bread and cup. They respond to God's call to minister to others—children, youth, and adults, who are a part of the community of faith—in ways similar to the care extended to widows and orphans by the early church. They nurture one another in the faith and in their relationship with Christ. They become "priests" to one another.

Ministry of the laity affirms the ministry each disciple has in the world. In these various ministries we use our God-given gifts as we respond to God's call to serve others in the name of Christ. The particular nature of the ministry varies greatly. It may be within the family as mother or father. It may be job-related, serving others in a business or a profession. It may be a call to volunteer service, providing needed support to the community and its members. It may be a call that has political implications or that leads to social action. Whatever its exact form, it begins with a stirring in the heart, as a sense of calling from God. When we are open, the Holy Spirit directs us into a particular role, not just because we want to be there, but because we believe that this is what God intends for us to do.

This understanding of the ministry of the laity is grounded in our Baptist principle of the priesthood of all believers. That principle maintains that each person stands before God; no roles elevate some above others. All can go directly to God and have a personal relationship with God without the need for another person to intercede. In the same way, all are called by God. Each one of us is called to a ministry that uses the gifts God has given us.

Each of us has both the freedom and the responsibility to exercise that ministry.

The implications for the congregation of this understanding of ministry of the laity are significant. This principle emphasizes the importance of the congregational role in helping members discover, develop, and use their gifts; implies that sensitivity to God's call is a primary concern for all Christians; and suggests that churches value their members' gifts and response to God's call to minister as laity in the church and the world!

Exploring the Biblical Basis

The New Testament offers no clear description or definition of ministry of the laity, because there was no formalized process of ordination, no separation of clergy and laity in the early church. Passages such as Ephesians 4:1–7, 11–13, however, provide a solid underpinning for this historic Baptist principle. They affirm three basic concepts that continue to be important for us today: (1) Christ gave a variety of gifts; (2) these gifts are to be used to enable others in ministry; and (3) this ministry belongs to all the people of God, both clergy and laity, and takes place both inside and outside the church.

The concern of Paul's letter to the Ephesians is nothing less than the redemption of all creation. You can't get much bigger in scope than that! In the letter's view, this is God's plan; it is also what the work of Christ was and is all about. As the body of Christ, the church continues that work. This is where the ministry of the laity comes in. The ministry of the *laos*, the people of God, is to join in the work of redemption, not just of themselves, but of all creation.

This is easier said than done. After this bold affirmation in Ephesians 1, much of the rest of the letter explains how this happens through the church and in the lives of Christians. Our focus passage in this session comes from the section of the letter that deals with the church. Immediately Paul acknowledges the call that comes to all Christians and encourages his readers to remain faithful to that call (4:1). He then affirms our unity in Christ: "one Lord, one faith, one baptism, one God and Father of all, who is above all and through all and in all." (4:5) This unity, however, is not sameness, for there is variety in the church, specifically a variety of gifts. In Ephesians these gifts are seen as different roles that are played in the church: some are apostles, some prophets, some evangelists, some pastors and teachers. All these are essential if the church is to fulfill its purpose. These roles exist "to equip the saints for the work of ministry, for building up the body of Christ" (4:12). Remember, the meaning of saints here is broader than simply those special people who have a particularly high degree of holiness or who have enabled miracles. It is the term used to describe *all* who have claimed Jesus Christ as their Lord and Savior, much as we might use the term *believer* or *disciple*. The meaning of this phrase, then, is that the various gifts exist so that disciples will be equipped to do the work of the church, for "ministry, for building up the body of Christ." These are really two sides of the same coin. Ministry and building up the body of Christ are so intimately tied together that they cannot be separated. The place and nature of this work entail a wide range of possibilities.

At the time the letter was written, there was no clear notion of ordination. The specific roles mentioned in the passage were for *everyone*, not just clergy. Any of the *laos* might be in the role of apostle, prophet, evangelist, pastor, or teacher. The key was whether or not they had the specific gifts needed to fulfill these roles. The primary focus of prophets, pastors, and teachers was most often inside the church. That of the apostles and evangelists, however, was most often outside. Similarly, the ministry of the saints could be both within the church or to the community and world. All of it was and is ministry. All of it led and leads to building up the body of Christ.

As you prepare for this lesson:

Pray for each youth by name. As you prepare for this week's session, think about the youths' gifts. Identify the ways they are using them. What may they say about the future direction of their lives? Have they talked with you about what God is calling them to do? Are they involved in volunteer efforts? Could this be a way God is calling them? As you pray for each person in the class, focus on the ways God may be calling him or her. Pray that each student may be more aware of that call and, through this session, may identify ways to faithfully participate in the work of Christ.

Read and reflect on the Bible passage. The fourth chapter of Ephesians is one of the more familiar passages among the New Testament letters. Don't let this familiarity keep you from prayerful reflection on it. If you have time, you may want to read the entire letter. If this is not possible, reading chapters 1–4 will help provide a setting for the specific passage we will be using in the session.

Beginning

1. **Hopes for the future.** (5–10 minutes)
   * Welcome the youth to class.
   * Tell the class that today you will be talking about the way God calls each of us to be involved in ministry. Baptists call this "ministry of the laity."
   * Distribute handout #7.
   * Ask the youth to complete the three sentences found on their handout under "Hopes for the Future."
   * When the class members have finished writing, ask them to share their response for the first sentence by going around the circle. Encourage those who might not want to share, but tell them that it is okay to "pass" if they so choose.
   * Inform the youth that you are going to give them three more incomplete statements to finish. Read them one at a time giving them time to record their

response on the handout. The statements are:

- Five years from now the most important thing God will want me to do is . . .
- Ten years from now God hopes that I will be . . .
- Twenty years from now God sees me . . .

- Ask these questions:
  1. How did your answers change? How did they stay the same?
  2. Which was easier to do: write your hopes for the future or God's hopes for you?
  3. Do you think God really has hopes for your future? Why or why not?

Exploring

2. **Three biblical calls.** (15–20 minutes)
   - Ask the youth to review "Questions for Life" on their handout.
   - Ask: "Could you answer all of these questions with 100 percent accuracy right now? Why or why not?"
   - Tell the youth that you are now going to look at three people from the Bible who were dealing with similar questions and whose lives changed because they heard a call from God.
   - Divide the class into three groups.
   - Assign to each group one of the three biblical characters from "When God Calls" on their handout.
   - Ask them to:
     - Read the introduction on the handout.
     - Look up the suggested Bible passages.
     - Develop a brief skit that reenacts the call, but in a contemporary setting with people and situations that occur today.
   - Allow about 10 minutes for preparation,

then call the class back together to share the skits.

- Once all three groups have completed their skits, facilitate a brief discussion using these or your own questions:
  1. Why do you think these three people said yes to God's call?
  2. Do you think God always calls you to do something that is difficult or something you don't want to do? Why or why not?
  3. Does God call people today? How do you think God does that?

3. **Ephesians 4.** (5–10 minutes)
   - Ask youth to turn to Ephesians 4 in their Bibles.
   - Use the material in "Exploring the Bible Basis" to briefly provide some background. Include these points:
     1. The letter begins by describing God's plan, which is the redemption of all creation—that is, bringing all creation back into relationship with God so that it can be the way God intended it to be. This is what the work of Christ was and is all about.
     2. This is also the work of the church, which is the body of Christ.
     3. All disciples of Christ have a role to play in this work.
     4. Ministry of the laity is a historic Baptist principle. *(See "Background for the Leader" for additional information.)*
   - Summarize by explaining that this passage talks in detail about how we as disciples play the role God intends for us.
   - Ask someone in the class to read Ephesians 4:1–7.
   - Explain that the beginning point here is call; Paul is encouraging us to be faithful to God's call to us. The rest of the passage talks about how we do that. *(Note that Paul then goes on to affirm the one great thing everyone in the church*

*has in common, faith in Christ [vv. 4–6].
He then begins to talk about an important way in which we are different,
which is in the gifts God has given us
[v. 7].)*

- Ask another person in the class to read Ephesians 4:11–13.
- Ask these questions:
  1. What are the gifts God has given? *(You might mention at this point that other New Testament passages mention even more gifts.)*
  2. How are these gifts to be used? *(Material from "Exploring the Biblical Basis" will be helpful. The main point of this discussion should be that God has given all of us gifts that enable us to respond to God's call to do the work of ministry. Hint: You may want to write this summary statement on newsprint or the chalkboard.)*

4. **Personal gifts and calls.** (5–10 minutes)
   - Ask youth to look at "God's Gifts" on the handout.
   - Read the brief description about gifts together.
   - Ask youth to complete the sentence, "I think some of my gifts are . . ."

5. **Recognizing other's gifts.** (10 minutes)
   - Say: "Often our real gifts are so much a part of us that we are not even aware of them."
   - Distribute blank pieces of paper and ask each youth to write his or her name in the center.
   - Say: "It is important to invite others to share with us about the gifts they see in us."
   - Instruct the youths to pass their papers to the left. The persons who receive the

papers will write a word or brief phrase about that person's gifts. Keep the papers moving to the left until they each return to the person whose name is in the center.

- Give the youth a few moments to read what others wrote on their paper.
- Read or paraphrase the description of call found in "God's Call" on the handout.
- Ask: "Do you sense God calling you?" *(Most youth are not accustomed to thinking about their lives in this way. If there is little response, simply encourage the youth to ask God to help them see their gifts and contribution in time.)*

Responding

6. **Hopes and prayers.** (5 minutes)
   - Review the key issues discussed today. Reflect on Moses', Jeremiah's, and Mary's calls. Note that some calls are like this while others are far less dramatic and grow out of work we are already doing. However the call comes to us, it is the Christian conviction that our lives are always lived most fully and meaningfully when we have heard and responded to what God wants us to do and be. This is ministry in its most important sense, a ministry of everyone who believes in Christ.
   - Close with prayer. Ask for sensitivity to the ways God calls us and courage to respond to that call.

Note

1. Loren Mead, *Five Challenges for the Once and Future Church* (Bethesda, MD: Alban Institute, 1996), 1–15.

8

Discipleship
Walking and Talking Like Jesus

Bible Basis:
Colossians 1:27–29

Objectives
At the end of the session youth will be able to:
- describe two key elements of the maturity of Jesus;
- state at least one way they will work to grow as disciples of Christ in next week.

Key Bible Verse:
". . . to bring each one into God's presence as a mature individual in union with Christ" (Colossians 1:28, TEV).

Background for the Leader

Christians believe in discipleship—that is, they believe that all who claim faith in Jesus Christ are called to learn about and follow in the way Christ teaches. Baptists, however, bring another dimension to this common belief. Baptists believe in the priesthood of all believers. This notion, that we all have both direct access to God and a ministry from God, makes discipleship an important part of our life and faith. It is through discipleship that our priestly role is developed and our ministry lived out.

A disciple of Jesus Christ seeks to learn more about Jesus and to practice what is learned each day. Discipleship is about knowing Christ, having a significant relationship with him, and living the way Christ would live. Discipleship incorporates all of our life—our being, our knowing, and our doing. This call to discipleship is set against the Baptist focus on

the priesthood of believers. Because God calls each one of us to a ministry, part of growing as a disciple is discovering and living out that call.

One way to understand discipleship is to think of it as three pieces of the same pie. Each slice is different, yet each one is connected to the other, and each one has pretty much the same ingredients as the other. The three pieces of the "discipleship pie" are *deepening spiritual life, equipping,* and *ministering.*

Deepening spiritual life speaks about the need for disciples to continue to grow in their personal relationship with Christ. Relationships always require work. A relationship with Christ is no different. In fact, in some ways, it may be more difficult because there is no flesh and blood person with whom we can sit down across a table and talk. What's great about this relationship is that Christ constantly seeks us out. Christ constantly loves us. Christ constantly desires to have a relationship with us. Spiritual disciplines are the ways Christians

33

traditionally seek to grow in their relationship with Jesus. From prayer to action, from meditation to Bible study, these disciplines are all about strengthening our relationship with Christ. As our relationship with Christ is strengthened, our spiritual life is deepened.

Equipping speaks of the need to continue to acquire the knowledge and skills that make faithful living possible. For Christians a key to equipping is found in the discovery and development of our God-given gifts. These gifts are given for ministry, to live out our lives as disciples of Jesus Christ. Being equipped, then, is the ongoing process of discovering and developing our gifts. Other important aspects of equipping include acquiring both knowledge and skills. To be disciples of Jesus Christ, we need to know who he is, what he teaches, and how we are to live. That knowledge comes primarily through Bible study. Living as faithful disciples may also require the use of particular skills, such as preaching, leadership, working with groups, carpentry, or cooking. The list is limitless and depends on the way in which we have been called to live out our discipleship.

Ministering speaks of the need to put faith into action. We do this when we respond to God's call to serve others in the name of Jesus Christ. The deepening spiritual life and the equipping both have a purpose—involvement in ministry as Christ's disciples. In ministering we are fulfilling our call and continuing to grow as disciples of Christ.

Exploring the Biblical Basis

Paul was in prison. Before him stood the stark reality that he might be put to death because of his work. He used this time to reflect on his life and ministry—the things he had been about and that were most important to him. The section of the Letter to the Colossians that is the Bible basis for this session comes from this part of his reflection.

In Colossians 1:24 (TEV) Paul talks about his suffering. He rejoices in it because it completes the suffering of Christ. As Christ suffered for the church, so Paul suffers for the church. His imprisonment is directly related to the work of the church. That work is, in a word, discipleship. It is bringing "each one into God's presence as a mature individual in union with Christ" (Colossians 1:28, TEV). The Greek word translated "mature" can also be translated "complete." We become mature as we complete God's intentions for us. This happens, Paul claims, through the proclamation of the "secret" that God has now revealed to everyone. The secret is this: "Christ is in you, which means that you will share the glory of God" (Colossians 1:27, TEV).

Through this indwelling Christ we become mature, and the work of discipleship is accomplished. For Paul this is an ongoing process. In his letter to the Philippians he refers to a race that is being run but is not yet completed (Philippians 3:12–14). Ephesians speaks of the time in the future when we will become "mature [people], reaching to the very height of Christ's full stature" (Ephesians 4:13, TEV). For now, however, the challenge is to keep growing as disciples.

Later in this section of Colossians Paul writes about how that happens. These verses are not included in the Bible basis for this session, but they are important to understanding the work of discipleship. "Since you have accepted Christ Jesus as Lord, live in union with him. Keep your roots deep in him, build your lives on him, and become ever stronger in your faith, as you were taught" (Colossians 2:6–7, TEV). These few words are rich in insights about discipleship.

1. Discipleship begins with our acceptance of Christ as Lord. Certainly we learn about being a disciple before then. What we learn helps us commit to Christ, but the actual process of discipleship begins once we have said yes to Christ's call and claim on our lives.

2. The central feature of discipleship is

learning to live in union with Christ. This is possible because Christ already dwells in us. We fulfill that union when we recognize it and begin to order our lives around it.

3. Keeping our roots deep in Christ is what enables the first element of discipleship as described in "Background for the Leader." This is what deepening spiritual life is all about.

4. The other two elements of discipleship, equipping and ministering, are encompassed in building our lives on Christ. This includes how we live out our faith in our relationships and what we choose to do with our lives.

5. Discipleship is not just sit-down-and-listen teaching. It also includes the teaching that comes from living our lives alongside other disciples and following Jesus as the model of what it means to be truly mature.

As you prepare for this lesson:

Pray for each youth by name. Discipleship is important for everyone in your class. Those who have made a commitment to Christ in baptism are already disciples. They need to be nurtured in their knowledge of what it means to be a disciple and in their ability to live as one. Those who have not yet made this commitment to Christ can begin to understand more fully what such a commitment means as they explore discipleship in this session. Focus on where each youth is in his or her relationship with Christ, especially as you pray for each one.

Read and reflect on the Bible passage. Read Colossians 1:27–29, the basis for this session. You may want to read the entire section this passage is taken from, Colossians 1:24–2:5, to give you a better sense of the context. Also, read Colossians 2:6–7 and consider its insights into the process of discipleship. Take time to reflect on the key elements that you believe are involved in being mature in Christ. How do you demonstrate these in your own life? What are the points at which you personally need to grow as a disciple of Christ?

Beginning

1. **Talk about "when I grow up."**
   (5–10 minutes)
   - Welcome the youth.
   - Ask:
     1. Have you ever been asked, "What do you want to be when you grow up?"
     2. How do you feel when someone asks you this question?
     3. What kind of answers do you typically give?
   - Explain that for the purpose of today's session you want them to think about a slightly different question.
   - Ask:
     1. What do you want to be *like* when you grow up?
     2. What do you think it would be like to be completely mature?
     3. Is "complete maturity" even possible?
   - Allow time for a few youth to share their thoughts about this.
   - Write their responses on newsprint or the chalkboard.

Exploring

2. **Read and discuss the Bible passage.**
   (5 minutes)
   - Use these or your own words to introduce the Bible passage: "Maturity is an important issue for Christians. In fact, it is one of the most important issues. We often understand maturity as becoming more like Jesus. This process of becoming more like Jesus is called discipleship."
   - Ask the youth to turn to Colossians 1: 27–29 in their Bibles.
   - Inform the youth that in this passage Paul is writing about the purpose of his ministry.
   - Ask them to listen for the way maturity is described.
   - Read the passage.

- Ask:
  1. What do you think it means to be "a mature individual in union with Christ?"
  2. How are the words we listed on the chalkboard (or newsprint) similar or different from Paul's understanding of maturity?

3. **Describe Jesus' maturity.**
(10–15 minutes)
- Say: "One way to understand the kind of maturity Paul is talking about is to look at Jesus. As we study his life and learn how he lived, we can see the qualities that are to be a part of our lives when we live in union with him."
- Divide the class into pairs.
- Distribute handout #8.
- Assign at least one of the following passages to each pair. All are from the Gospel of Luke:

2:41–50	7:11–15
4:1–13	8:22–25
4:16–30	18:15–17
4:42–44	19:1–10
5:27–32	22:28–42

- Ask them to read the passage and to determine what quality or qualities of Jesus the passage is illustrating. *(Tell youth to focus on the quality that Jesus is demonstrating rather than on the action itself, since many of these are miracles that could not be duplicated by the youth.)*
- Ask youth to write next to the appropriate passage on their handout the qualities illustrated.
- After 5 minutes bring the group together.
- Ask the youth to share the qualities they found.
- Add them to the list you wrote on newsprint or the chalkboard.

4. **Share "more likely" skits.**
(10–15 minutes)
- Explain that it is one thing to recognize Jesus as a model of maturity but

something very different to actually live that way.
- Divide the class into two groups.
- Ask each group to select one of the passages you have looked at. They are to develop a brief skit that depicts what might more likely happen if a similar incident were to occur today and an average person, not Jesus, were involved.
- Allow about five minutes for them to develop the skits.
- Invite each group to share their skit.
- Facilitate a brief discussion using these or your own questions:
  1. What was "real" about each skit? How so?
  2. Was there anything you wouldn't do but could see someone you know doing? What? Say more about why you wouldn't do it but why you could see someone else doing it.
  3. If you had an opportunity to do what was done in the skit in real life, would you? Why or why not?

5. **Complete a discipleship profile.**
(10 minutes)
- Use the material in "Background for the Leader" to introduce the three elements of discipleship: spiritual growth, equipping, and ministering.
- Ask the youth to turn to "My Discipleship Profile" on the handout.
- Instruct them to take a few minutes to complete their profile.
- Explain that they can write anything they want. The profile will not be shared with the class unless they choose to share something they wrote.
- When they are done, ask:
  1. Was that easy or hard to do?
  2. What was easy? Why?
  3. What was hard? Why?
  4. Are there any you weren't sure about? *(If so, explore their questions so that they might complete their profile later.)*

Responding

6. **Decide on next steps.** (5 minutes)
   - Ask youth to review the profile they developed and the list of mature qualities from early steps in the session.
   - Ask them to select one area in which they would like to grow in their own discipleship and to write their response on their handout.
   - After a few moments ask them to select one quality they would like to strengthen and to write their response on their handout.

   - Then ask them to write one thing they will do during the coming week to strengthen that quality.

7. **Close with prayer.** (5 minutes)
   - Ask the group to gather in prayer.
   - Explain that you will begin the prayer by sharing the area you have set to work on during the coming week. Invite those who wish to share their goal for the week to do the same, either silently or aloud.
   - When everyone has shared, pray for God's guidance and strength to help everyone grow as a disciple of Jesus Christ.

9

Evangelism
Sharing the Good News

Bible Basis:
Acts 3:1–16

Objectives
At the end of the session youth will be able to:

• identify "good news" as something that is meant to be shared;
• identify one person with whom they will share the Good News of Jesus Christ;
• describe one way they can share the Good News of Jesus Christ.

Key Bible Verse:
"I have no silver or gold, but what I have I give you; in the name of Jesus Christ of Nazareth, stand up and walk" (Acts 3:6).

Background for the Leader

It is difficult to think about Baptists without thinking about evangelism. Before receiving believer's baptism, a person experiences the transforming power of Jesus Christ and makes a commitment to follow him. With this experience comes joy, forgiveness, liberation, and a new sense of meaning and purpose. Because these new feelings and experiences need to be talked about, there comes a desire to share. But the sharing is also a witness so that others may know this great experience too. That's what evangelism is all about. And that's why evangelism is so basic to being a Baptist.

It is often said that Baptists became a denomination because of mission. Our first national organizational structure, the American Baptist Foreign Mission Society, was formed to support the work of Adoniram and Ann Judson in Burma. The American Baptist Home Mission Society was formed to support mission efforts of people like John Mason Peck on the American frontier. When the Woman's American Baptist Home Mission Society was formed, its first missionary was Joanna P. Moore, already at work among the freed slaves of the American South. It might just as easily be said, however, that Baptists formed denominations because of evangelism, for evangelism was the primary focus of this mission work. The passion to share the Good News with others motivated the Judsons, Peck, Moore, and all those who supported them through the formation of these mission organizations. As Baptists, evangelism has been and still is basic to us.

Just as our understanding of mission has expanded from those early days, so has our understanding of evangelism. In recent years American Baptists have been guided by this definition of evangelism, which was adopted by their General Board in June 1984:

Evangelism is
   the joyous witness of the People of God
      to the redeeming love of God
   urging all to repent
   and to be reconciled to God and each other
   through faith in Jesus Christ
      who lived, died, and was raised from the
         dead,
so that
   being made new
   and empowered by the Holy Spirit
   believers are incorporated as disciples into
      the church
      for worship, fellowship, nurture and
         engagement in God's mission
            of evangelism and liberation within
               society and creation,
            signifying the Kingdom which is present
               and yet to come.

That's a pretty inclusive statement. At its core, however, is the sharing of the Good News of Jesus Christ. Despite changes in approach over the years, despite differing styles, that has been and still is what evangelism is all about.

Like mission, our understanding of evangelism needs to be shaped today by the relatively new and all-important reality that the majority of the society in which we live has no ongoing relationship with a church. In the past we had a tendency to think about evangelism as something we do with "them"—people who are different from us. After all, nearly everyone who was like us was already involved in a church! That is no longer the case. This reality calls for an understanding of evangelism that moves beyond the mass event and into personal relationships. A new view of evangelism moves away from a single transforming experience to an ongoing process of being transformed. It calls for *each of us* to develop a renewed commitment to and understanding of the ways in which we are and can be evangelists.

Exploring the Biblical Basis

Peter was new at the practice we now call evangelism. After all, only a few weeks had passed since Pentecost, when he and others had been sent into the world to share the Good News of Jesus Christ. It must have been a challenge for him to respond correctly, to share appropriately, to help others see the new reality that had so shaped his own life. He might very well have dealt with all the same issues that confront us when it comes to being evangelists.

His interaction with the beggar at the temple, which is the biblical text for this session, was no exception. He was in a new situation that called for a new response. But Peter, led by the Holy Spirit, came through. He responded in a way that enabled faith. In doing so he provided us with a number of important insights about what it means to be an evangelist, insights we can apply to our own lives.

Peter understood that the gospel comes to people as a response to human need. The declared need was money. The deeper need was healing. The still deeper need was salvation. It was to the need for healing that Peter responded, even though that wasn't what the man was asking for. It is possible that the man's reason for not asking for healing was a belief that it was impossible.

Perhaps Peter recalled Jesus responding to a crippled man by saying, "Your sins are forgiven" (Mark 2:1–12). But Peter's response was not quite so bold. He chose to meet the man at a level of need that was both real and deep.

Peter understood what he could offer and what he couldn't. At least part of Peter's response to the man was based on understanding what he could provide and what he couldn't. Peter offered what he could, and with and through the power of the Holy Spirit, it was enough. Perhaps from the man's perspective it was more than enough. As we share the Good News we must remember that the gospel doesn't solve all problems the way people would like to have them solved. There are some things we can provide and other things that we must leave to God's infinite wisdom.

Peter was willing to risk in order make the Good News real. The risk for Peter came in at least two ways. First, there was the risk that healing would not come. The claim Peter made was a bold one made in faith. But every act of boldness is a risk. We risk that somehow we may have misread God's intention or misunderstood our purpose. We risk failing to do what we said we would do. In addition to the risk of failure, there was for Peter, and also for us, a second risk, the risk of consequence. The consequence for Peter, within a short period of time, was jail. There are, even in the twenty-first century, consequences when we share the Good News with others.

Peter was clear about the power behind the Good News. In conversation with those who witnessed the healing and speeches before his accusers, Peter clearly declared the source of the power that healed. It wasn't him or the act of healing itself that was important; it was the declaration of what that power was. The power of God is what makes healing possible. The power of God is the Good News. Evangelists speak and are empowered by this power.

Peter understood that all people have complete freedom to respond or not respond to the Good News. Peter had a clear understanding of his role: it was to bring healing and to explain the source of that healing power. What the beggar, the witnesses, and his accusers did with that was not up to him. It was between them and God.

As you prepare for this lesson:

Pray for each youth by name. We all continually need to be evangelized. We always need to hear Christ's word for us so that we can be brought into closer relationship with God. What word do you need to hear? Think about the members of your class. What might your evangelistic role with them be this week? Pray that you will know the word that needs to be shared with each of them. Ask God to help you reveal to these students the healing nature of Jesus who is among us by the Holy Spirit. Pray that they may develop a greater sense of themselves as evangelists.

Read and reflect on the Bible passage.

Read Acts 3:1–16. If you have time and would like to set these events in the broader context of the days following Pentecost, read Acts 2:1–4:31. Reflect on your own role as an evangelist. Is it one with which you are comfortable? In what ways do you need to grow in that role? Your willingness to share about this with the class will increase their openness.

Beginning

1. **Share "good news" stories.** (5–10 minutes)
   - Welcome the youth as they arrive.
   - Tell the youth a good news story from your life or use this example:
     "A mission-support friend, from an affluent church on the other side of town, called with some good news. The household belongings of a person who died were being given to 'where they would do the most good.' In our church's neighborhood—a mixed blue-collar, working poor, and low-income neighborhood—people struggle to make ends meet. That's why we received the phone call! Recently, one family had a house fire. They can use some of the items we will retrieve from this estate. Another family's parents both work, but they can't always give their children with learning disabilities everything they need. There might be some things from the estate to share with them too! As the pastor of this small American Baptist church, it is good news to see how God brings together the resources we need to give our neighbors a lift!"
   - Distribute handout #9.
   - Ask for volunteers to tell a good news story.
   - Coach their storytelling as needed.

Exploring

2. **Define evangelism.** (5–10 minutes)
   - Generate a brief discussion using these or your own questions:

1. What is it like to hear good news stories?
2. Which do you prefer, to tell good news stories or to listen to good news stories?
3. Sometimes we refer to the Bible as the Good News. To what "Good News" are we referring? (*Encourage the youth to tell you the story of Christ's birth, life, death, and resurrection.*)
4. What does evangelism mean?
5. Congratulate the youth for being evangelists. (*They just evangelized you by telling you the Good News of Jesus Christ!*)

- Briefly review *American Heritage Dictionary's* definition of evangelism from the handout.
- Using your own words, say: "I believe there's more to evangelism, or telling the Good News, than that. Our Bible study today will help us get a clearer grasp of the idea and practice of evangelism. So will the Statement on Evangelism printed on your student handout, which was developed by a team of American Baptist pastors and church leaders. As you look at this statement, what does it tell you about Baptists and evangelism?"
- Ask the youth to note the Key Bible Verse. Remind them it's from Acts 3:6, today's lesson.

3. **Read the Bible story.** (10–15 minutes)
- Ask the class to turn in their Bibles to Acts 3:1–16. Use the material in "Exploring the Biblical Basis" to set the scene for the story they are about to read. Ask for a volunteer or volunteers to read the passage.
- Use the following comments and questions to guide a discussion: "This lesson consists of two main sections: first, the story of the healing of the lame man, and second, Peter's message in the temple. (*This is often called the second Christian sermon, the first being Peter's message in Acts 2, following the Pentecost gift of the Holy Spirit.*) Let's talk first about the healing story. What do you think it might have been like for the person who couldn't walk, who had to rely on family and friends to carry him to the gate of the temple so he could beg for money?"
- Say: "When the lame man asked for money, two things typically happened. Some people, with a small bit of compassion, would drop a coin in his hand and keep on moving. Many others would pretend to not even recognize him and quickly move past him."
- Ask:
  1. What did Peter and John do? (*They looked straight at him and said, "Look up at us!"*)
  2. Why do you think they said that?
  3. How did the lame man who was healed react? How would you react?
  4. What exactly did Peter say to the lame man? (*Give them time to find verse 5 and read it.*)
  5. Why did he say, "I have no silver or gold"? Why would he clarify what he could not give to the man when he had something so much better to give?
  6. What difference does it make in the story that, after saying to the lame man, "Get up and start walking," Peter also took him by the right hand and helped him up?
  7. If the man was being healed, why would he need a helping hand? What does that gesture signify? What does it add to the story?
  8. Were there any "helping hands" in the good news stories you shared with one another today?
  9. Who might be some people today

that remind us of this man? Explain.

10. What could you, like Peter and John, do or say to them?

4. **Discover key points of the Good News.** (10–15 minutes)

- Say: "Sometimes it's hard to do or say anything to another person about our faith because others are watching and, perhaps, judging us. Look again at verses 11–16, Peter's message in the temple. *(Give the students time to review these verses.)* One important feature of Peter's message is called *'the kerygmatic proclamation.'* That's a biblical scholar's fancy term for saying, 'This is the central message that we Christians, as followers of Jesus, our risen Lord, have to share with the world, about him.' Bible scholars have looked through the New Testament very carefully trying to figure out what important points to lift up when sharing the Christian message, the Good News. These verses contain elements of that essential list. Let's decipher them."

- Divide the class into four small groups. Assign verse 13 to one group, verse 14 to the second, verse 15 to the third, and verse 16 to the fourth. Ask each group to read their verse and to record on a sheet of paper the important point (or points) Peter says about Jesus Christ's life, death, and resurrection.

- Bring the class back together. Ask each group to report the significant point(s) they recorded. List the points on the chalkboard or newsprint. Compare these to the points listed on the handout. Then use the following questions to guide a discussion:

1. What could you see yourself saying and why?

2. What can't you see yourself saying and why?

3. What could you say instead?

Responding

5. **Decide how to share the Good News.** (5–10 minutes)

- Ask:

1. What "contemporary" words or stories could we use to share the Good News about Jesus with our friends and family?

2. Using these points as guidelines, what are some realistic ways in which you can share the Good News of Jesus Christ?

- Ask the youth to write in their handout the name or names of people with whom they would like to share the Good News of Jesus Christ.

- Suggest that they pray for each name on their list during the coming week.

- Teach them to pray using your own or the following prayer suggestion: "Dear God, Please guide me to a time and a place where I can share with [friend's name] a story about knowing you. Help me to share with [him/her] the joy I have found in knowing Jesus! Help [him/her] to want that joy too. In Jesus' name I pray. Amen."

- Summarize by saying: "As Baptists we believe in evangelism! We believe in telling Good News stories. So let's do some storytelling this week!"

- Lead the youth in a closing prayer. Lift up the call that is upon all Christians to share the Good News of Jesus Christ! Pray for the courage to share the Good News. Thank God for the privilege of having such a great story to share.

10

Worship and Communion
Dead or Alive?

Bible Basis:
Psalm 95:1–7a

Objectives

At the end of the session youth will be able to:

- name at least three qualities of worship that make it exciting and meaningful to them;
- identify at least two ways the elements of worship happen in their life outside of church;
- experience a sacred dimension of corporate worship more fully.

Key Bible Verse:

"O come, let us worship and bow down, let us kneel before the LORD, our Maker!" (Psalm 95:6).

Background for the Leader

Ideas about worship abound! There may be as many "Baptist" styles of worship as there are Baptist churches! With no prayer book to guide us, no book of order to govern us, each congregation makes its own decisions about worship. Everything from liturgical formality to charismatic spontaneity happens in Baptist churches. And sometimes both happen in the same Baptist church!

With so many possibilities before us, there is bound to be a healthy disagreement about what is best. There are also, from time to time at least, bound to be outright battles over what happens in the worship service. Even whether or not to sing "Amen" at the end of hymns can be a bone of contention! These disagreements testify to the important role worship plays in our lives. It truly is sacred.

If worship is sacred, it is also in many ways personal. At least that's the way people often approach it. The question many use to evaluate worship is simply, "Was it meaningful to me?" Personal meaning is important, of course, but it is not the whole story. Worship is a *corporate* experience, something for the people of God gathered together as a community of faith. The *we* of worship is just as important, if not more important, than the *me* of worship. The focus of worship is God, so rather than "What did I get out of it?" a more appropriate question to ask might be "What did God get out of it?" That question is certainly more difficult to answer, but asking it can, at the very least, help us keep the focus of worship in the right place.

Recent studies of worship and the role it plays in our lives reveal some interesting information. In most churches there seems to be a generational difference in what is seen as "good" worship. One study captured this difference in two simple words. Those born prior to World War II think of worship primarily as *meditation*. Those born following that war think of it primarily as *celebration*. Both are important to worship, but a view of what is *most* important shapes attitudes on a whole array of worship issues. If worship is primarily meditation, a quiet time for personal preparation before worship is essential. But if it is primarily celebration, a joyous time of community sharing makes sense. If worship is meditation, children can be a disruption. But if it is celebration, children help set the proper tone. If worship is meditation, a sermon that prompts personal contemplation is just right. But if it is celebration, that same sermon can destroy the essential mood. If worship is meditation, prayers of confession play a central role. But if it is celebration, prayers of thanksgiving are most important.

Despite significant personal differences and great differences in worship practices among Baptist churches, there are several important common affirmations we can make. Each of these is related to the heritage we share as Baptists.

1. The differences that exist among us result from one of our most basic principles—the autonomy of the local congregation. This is why there is no prayer book, no prescribed form of worship for all to follow.

2. The centrality of the Bible in our life and faith is another Baptist principle that shapes our worship. The reading of God's Word and proclamation based on that Word are significant emphases of Baptist worship, even though the style of worship may vary greatly.

3. Because we believe in the priesthood of all believers, the proclamation of God's Word deals with living as faithful "priests" in today's world.

4. Our understanding of the ordinances of baptism and Communion also provide a common thread for our approach to worship. The similarity in the practice of these two ordinances in Baptist churches is an affirmation of the common heritage we share. The regular gathering at the Lord's Table affirms our unity despite differences. No matter the particular understanding of Communion we bring to that table, we also affirm that Christ is the one who brings us there, and he alone truly unites us.

Exploring the Biblical Basis

Psalm 95 is one of the most familiar of all the psalms. It is a joyous expression of praise to God for who he is and what he has done. It expresses in a minimum of words what true worship is all about.

This psalm uses a repeating pattern to call God's people into a worshiping relationship. Verses 1–2 present the invitation: "O come, let us sing to the Lord. . . ." Verses 3–5 remind listeners why this is the right thing to do: "For the Lord is a great God, and a great King above all gods. . . ." That pattern is then repeated. Verse 6 offers the invitation, "O come, let us worship and bow down . . . ," and verse 7 tells us why, "For he is our God. . . ."

Verses 1 and 2 suggest several important elements of our worshiping relationship with God. Singing, joy, thanksgiving, and praise are all parts of worship. The psalm calls us to worship, and worship is doing these things. We are important in worship, it seems to say, because of what we offer to God, not because of what is offered to us.

The reasons for worship provided in verses 3–5 and verse 7 offer another insight. Part of worship is remembering what God has done so that we can know who God is. God has created all things (the depths of the earth, the heights of the mountains, the sea, the dry land). God has cared for us and continues to care (as a shepherd cares for sheep). That is what God has done for us, that is who God is, and that is why we worship God.

Another important insight here is that God is "a great King above all gods." At first that seems like a strange affirmation for a psalm to make. After all, one of the most basic affirmations of our faith is that there is only one God. Why then do we go out of our way to say God is above all other gods? What other gods? This psalm was written in a time of competing gods, each demanding to be the object of worship. Times haven't changed. Back then they called them gods. Today it's more subtle, but many things still compete for our allegiance, things we are tempted to make the object of our living. We place our trust in things, looking to them for security, believing they will offer us purpose and peace. We worship those things instead of God. When we are called to worship, we must remember that God is above all other gods of our own making.

As you prepare for this lesson:

Pray for each youth by name. This session is about encountering the holy in our lives. When we talk about worship and what makes it meaningful, we are truly treading on sacred ground. Youth may be reluctant to share about this dimension of their lives, but it is still an important one. Your challenge as a teacher will be to help them become more aware of the sacred dimension of their lives and to understand that worship enables them to experience this dimension more fully. They may have found traditional worship to be less than meaningful, which may create additional resistance. As you prepare for this session, offer prayers for individual students as they encounter the "holy" in their lives. Pray for help to develop and lead a session that will enable them to deepen their experience of this encounter in their own lives and together as a worshiping community.

Read and reflect on the Bible passage. You might want to use this psalm as the basis for your own devotional experience during the days before the class session. These words are very familiar. Sometimes familiarity blinds us to the full richness of meaning to be found in a passage. Read this passage over several times slowly. Focus on key words. Find a different translation to read from. As you read the psalm, think about ways the elements of worship that are mentioned happen in your own life.

Consider a Communion Service

Communion is suggested as part of the worship service youth will be developing in this session. If you want to do this, talk with the pastor and any others in your church who are responsible for worship. Perhaps one of them will need to be there, as is true in some churches. In other churches the youth themselves may be able to lead this part of the service. In thinking about this option, consider youth who are not members of the church. It is important not to make them feel excluded if they are unable to share in Communion. For this reason it may be best simply to talk about the meaning of Communion as a part of the service.

Beginning

1. **"Dead" and "alive" times.** (10 minutes)
   - Welcome the youth.
   - Tell them that you want to begin the session today by exploring times they felt "dead" and "alive." Explain that you are not using these two terms literally, but as words to describe feelings of boredom, low energy, and purposelessness (dead) or excitement, high energy, and strong motivation (alive).
   - Ask youth to imagine there is a line on the floor. (Or make one by putting masking tape on the floor.)
   - Designate one end of the line the "dead" end and the other end the "alive" end.
   - Explain that you will name several activities in which they are involved. For each one they are to stand along the line based on how "dead" or "alive" they

feel while doing that activity. *(If, for example, they have little feeling at all about a certain activity, they would stand in the middle. If the activity is somewhat exciting for them, they would move toward the "alive" end. If they find the activity boring, they would stand near the "dead" end.)*

- Use these activities and add ones that you know are part of your students' lives:
  - going to a school basketball (or football or soccer or other popular sport) game
  - studying for a math test
  - watching MTV
  - having dinner with your family
  - going to a party with friends
  - visiting relatives
  - getting your driver's license
  - going to a youth group retreat
  - attending the Sunday morning worship service
- Ask youth to call out a few more activities.
- Invite students back to their seats.
- Ask: "What makes an activity 'dead' or 'alive'?"
- List student responses on newsprint or the chalkboard.
- Ask: "What specifically makes the Sunday morning worship service 'dead' or 'alive' for you?"
- List their reasons on newsprint or the chalkboard.

Exploring

2. **Experience Psalm 95.** (5 minutes)
   - Distribute handout #10.
   - Ask youth to read Psalm 95 out loud in unison.
   - Explain that this was written by someone who was excited about worship. It is an invitation to others to join in praising God. Point out that verses 1–2 and 6 issue the invitation and verses 3–5 and 7 explain why they should respond.
   - Divide the class into two groups.
   - Explain that you would like them to read the Psalm again but this time responsively.
   - Assign one group the odd-numbered verses and the other group the even-numbered verses.
   - Ask them to express the excitement the psalm writer had about worship in the way they read it.
   - Have them read the psalm responsively.
   - After they read it once, encourage them to do it once more.
   - Affirm their enthusiasm (even if it seems a bit wild). If their reading lacked excitement, encourage them to put more into it one last time.

3. **What makes worship "alive"?** (5–10 minutes)
   - Write these two partial sentences at the top of sheets of newsprint or on the chalkboard: "Worship is alive for me when . . ." and "Worship is dead for me when . . ."
   - Ask the youth to offer suggestions for completing each of the sentences.
   - Write these in the appropriate place and then discuss them with the class. *(Try to avoid a negative emphasis. If negative statements are offered, explore the positive side as well. If they don't like the music, for example, explore the kind of music they would like.)*

4. **Create worship experiences.** (15–20 minutes)
   - Tell the class that you would now like them to use the ideas they have come up with to create a time of worship that they will lead to conclude the class.
   - Ask the youth to look at the sections of "Creating a Worship Experience for Your Class" on the handout.

- Review the suggestions that are offered there for developing a worship service.
- Divide into groups, assigning one element of the worship service to each group. *(If your class is small, it would be possible to have one person work on the paraphrase of Psalm 95 and the prayer. Developing the "message" and preparing the music could be done more effectively with several students working together. Those working on music will have two sections, the Song of Praise and the Song of Affirmation of Commitment, to consider. Give them "Take a Stand!" or another youth music resource to use in their work. If you have a topical concordance, make it available to those who are working on the "message.")*
- Circulate among the groups, offering encouragement freely and suggestions only as requested. *(Although there is only a limited amount of time for preparation, it should be enough to do the work that is necessary.)*

Responding

5. **Worship.** (10–15 minutes)
   - Bring the groups together.
   - Remind the class that God is the focus of worship. They are not performing what they have done for each other. God is the real audience for any worship service.
   - Participate in the youth-led worship experience in the order presented on the handout.
   - In your own words, tell this story from our Baptist history: "As Baptists we have a long history of being concerned about worship. Back in the seventeenth century a man by the name of Obadiah Holmes journeyed from his home in Rhode Island to visit a friend who lived in Massachusetts. While there he helped lead a worship service in his friend's home. For that he was arrested, tried, convicted and received twenty lashes. While we don't have to prove it by getting ourselves whipped, I hope that worship still holds the importance for us that it did for him! It is vital for all of us to know what makes worship come alive for us and to worship in those ways."
   - Thank the youth for their good work.

Note: This session may provide the beginning work for a youth-led worship service for your entire congregation. If the youth have been involved during the session and their work demonstrates a genuine interest in making worship come alive for them, explore this possibility with your pastor. If the response is positive, suggest the possibility to the class.

11

Issues of Faith
Take a Stand!

Bible Basis:
Acts 4:23–31

Objectives
At the end of this session youth will be able to:

- tell what Peter and Amos's experiences say about taking a stand;
- identify two reasons why it may be difficult to take a stand;
- identify two reasons why, even though difficult, it might be necessary to take a stand.

Key Bible Verse:
"When they had prayed . . . they were all filled with the Holy Spirit and spoke the word of God with boldness" (Acts 4:31).

Background for the Leader

Christians are called to share God's Word with others. We do this by living out and talking about our faith. We do this as individuals, as a church, and as denominations.

Youth are aware of the many problems that exist in our world. Some know that the gospel calls us to take a stand related to many of these problems. And some, through their own experience, have learned that sometimes the way people respond to difficult situations is not shaped by the love of the gospel. Whether the problem is as sweeping as racism or as common as making fun of another youth, showing God's love means something concrete.

From our earliest days, Baptists have taken stands on issues of faith. Early Baptists learned that taking a stand on issues can be a difficult thing to do. Obadiah Holmes was whipped in Massachusetts for speaking God's Word in a worship service held in a friend's home. Other Baptists were ridiculed and jailed for speaking in opposition to state-supported churches. Despite the difficulties, the Baptist tradition of taking a stand continues today in local churches, in regional gatherings, and in national denominational meetings.

This is not an easy thing to do. Sometimes God's word for a particular situation or issue is not clear. Sometimes people of deep faith disagree over what that word might be. Sometimes we do not say anything because we are not clear what word needs to be spoken.

Despite the difficulty and disagreements, Christians are called to speak boldly. Baptist history contains many examples of people who boldly spoke God's Word. Isaac Backus spoke boldly for the separation of church and state. Prudence Crandall boldly established a school for African American women in Connecticut before the Civil War. Helen Barrett Montgomery was the first woman member of the Rochester, New York, school board, the first woman president of American Baptists, and a translator of the New Testament in a time when women did not do such things. Edwin Dahlberg boldly spoke against the evil of war. Jennie Clare Adams boldly served in a Philippine hospital and was killed with several other missionaries during World War II. Martin Luther King Jr. spoke eloquently and boldly of a dream he had for all God's people. Individual boldness is not easy. It is a great responsibility. Sometimes it is hard to discern the difference between our opinion and God's word. Sometimes we falsely assume that God has no word to speak because we can't "hear" one. Sometimes, like Jonah, we run and hide.

Our tradition as Baptists inspires and challenges us to speak God's Word boldly— even when it is difficult, even when the response may not be positive. As people of faith we have a responsibility to interpret and proclaim, to witness, and to defend the mighty works God is doing in our world.

This session will give you and your class the opportunity to consider ways in which you can remain true to this heritage, both as individuals and as a church.

Exploring the Biblical Basis

Things were not going well for the disciples. Immediately following Pentecost there had been a great burst of enthusiasm and many converts. It seemed that no power on earth would be able to stop the spread of the Good News. The believers eagerly gathered together to share their meals, to join in prayer, to worship, and to learn from the apostles. When they went out into the world, they couldn't keep silent. Transformed by their new faith, they were compelled to tell others how God's power had made a difference in their lives. That was what got them into trouble.

The trouble began when Peter and John healed a crippled beggar at the temple gate. (See session 9, "Evangelism," for a more detailed study of this story.) Peter made it worse by explaining to the crowd that the power that enabled this healing was the same power that raised the Jesus they had crucified from the dead. Such talk did not sit well with the temple authorities, so they had Peter and John arrested. With a stern warning to never again speak or teach in the name of Jesus, Peter and John were released from prison.

The Bible basis for this session relates the events that occurred immediately following Peter and John's return to the other believers. They told their story; then with the others, they prayed that they might be able to speak God's Word with boldness. The passage reports that their prayer was answered. The room in which they were gathered shook, and they were filled with the Holy Spirit and spoke the Word of God with boldness.

What would you do if you had been arrested and spent the night in jail? What would you do if you were threatened by the authorities and then released on the condition that you never speak or teach again? What *would* you do? Like Peter, John, and the other believers, we might pray. But would our prayers be for boldness? Thanksgiving, perhaps, for our deliverance. Protection, perhaps, so that such a thing would not happen again. But boldness— to speak God's Word even more boldly? This is a great prayer indeed!

It always takes boldness to speak God's Word. Even though it is a word of salvation based in God's great love for us, it often does not always sit well with those who hear it. Peter learned that early. And anyone who speaks God's Word knows that Peter's experience is not unique. Have you known this experience?

As you prepare for this lesson:

Pray for each youth by name. The value of this session is directly related to the way it speaks to the individual needs and interests of the youth in your class. Pray for them as you prepare. Remembering their faces, their lives, and their needs, ask God's Spirit to be with them during the week and when you gather for this session.

Read and reflect on the Bible passage. For further background on the events described in this passage, read Acts 3:1–4:22. It is a great story filled with drama and excitement. Try to become familiar enough with it that you can tell it in your own words for your class. Also read Amos 4:1–3; 5:11–15, 21–24. Become familiar with the words he used to take a stand against the poverty of his nation.

Special Materials

- The song "Take a Stand!" (found in the American Baptist youth music resource *Take a Stand!*) is suggested for use in this session. The resource includes a CD, music, and lyrics. You may request a free copy (while they last) by contacting Judson Press customer service at: 1-800-4JUDSON.

Beginning

1. **"Take a Stand!"** (5 minutes)
   - Play "Take a Stand!" as the youth arrive.
   - Distribute handout #11.
   - Ask youth to look at the words of the song printed on the handout.
   - Ask:
     1. What do you think the song is trying to say? *(We need to stand up for what we believe in. We need to do God's work in the world. The things we do make a difference in the world.)*
     2. The song was written by a Baptist. In what way(s) is this song a reflection of Baptist identity? *(Explain, if they have not already said so, that God has a work for each one of us to do and a word for each one of us to speak.)*

- Tell the students that in this session we will look at two biblical people and examine what their experience says about taking a stand both personally and as a group of Christians in the church. We will also begin to explore the way(s) God wants us to act as we encounter various situations in life.

Exploring

2. **Peter took a stand.** (5–10 minutes)
   - Ask: "Who was Peter?" *(He was a fisherman, one of Jesus' twelve disciples, an important apostle in the early church.)*
   - Briefly retell the events in Peter's life that are talked about in Acts 3:1–4:22. *(It is a story of great drama and excitement, so tell it that way!)* Include these key points:
     - Right after the beginning of the church, Peter and other early Christians in Jerusalem continued to go the temple every day to pray.
     - A blind beggar regularly sat at the temple gate asking for money from those who came to pray.
     - Rather than give him money, Peter healed him in the name of Jesus Christ.
     - Peter then went on to explain that the power that healed the man was the same power that had raised Jesus Christ, whom they had crucified, from the dead.
     - The religious authorities responded to Peter's teaching by putting him in jail for the night.
     - The next morning they called Peter before them, and after giving him a stern warning to never preach or heal in Jesus' name again, let him go.
   - Ask: "If you were Peter, what would you do next?" *(Possible responses: Go back*

to the temple to heal and preach. Leave town. Go back to fishing in Galilee. Hide for a while, at least until things blew over.)

- Tell the class that the Bible says that Peter prayed.
- Ask:
  1. Does that surprise you? Why or why not?
  2. Assuming you were like Peter and started praying, what would you pray for? *(Possible responses: Thank God for getting away; for changing the minds and hearts of the temple authorities; for protection from further troubles.)*
- Ask the class to read Acts 4:23–31 to find out what Peter really did pray for.
- Use the following questions or some of your own to facilitate a brief discussion about Peter's prayer:
  1. What did he pray for? *(Boldness!)*
  2. Boldness for what? *(He prayed for boldness to keep on preaching God's Word.)*
  3. What do you think of that?
  4. What kind of faith would it take to keep on preaching about Jesus right after you had been in jail for doing precisely that?
- Reiterate that Peter was one person who was not afraid to take a stand.

3. **Amos took a stand.** (5–10 minutes)
   - Tell the youth that you are going to take a look at a person from the Old Testament who was not afraid to take a stand.
   - Ask them to look at the handout and read "Amos: Up Close and Personal."
   - Ask:
     1. What similarities and differences do you see between that time and today?
     2. What might Amos say, to take a stand on God's side, about this situation in Israel?

- Ask youth to read Amos 4:1–3; 5:11–15, 21–24 to discover what he really did say.
- Ask:
  1. What did Amos mean by the phrase "you cows of Bashan"? *(He was referring to the wives of the rich leaders who were concerned only about their own comfort and luxuries. Note also that the reference in verse 3 to "Harmon" probably means a garbage dump.)*
  2. What reactions do you think Amos's words might have caused?
- Note that Amos speaks both words of condemnation (4:1–3; 5:11–13, 21–23) and words that tell what God is really seeking from the people (5:14–15, 24).

4. **Our turn to take a stand.** (10–15 minutes)
   - Explain to the class that, just like Peter and Amos did, we live in a world that needs to hear God's Word.
   - Say: "Not only is the world still this way, but God hasn't changed either. God is counting on people of faith to continue in the tradition of Amos and Peter. We do that as individuals as we try to discover and share the words that God wants us to speak to others. We also do that together with other people of faith. As Baptists, one of our characteristics is the desire to follow in Peter and Amos's footsteps and continue to speak God's Word on issues that are important to our faith and world."
   - Ask the youth to look at the "Should We Take a Stand?" section of the handout.
   - Ask them to work individually for a few moments to decide what issues they believe are important to speak on—as individuals and as a church.
   - Ask them to share their answers.
   - Facilitate a brief discussion following each issue. Note the issues that create the most discussion for the following step.

5. **Decide what stand to take.**
   (10–15 minutes)

   (Use the following to guide your explanation of the resolutions process that is typical in most Baptist denominations, or gather the information you need about your own denomination's specific process. This explanation is based on the process used by the American Baptist Churches in the U.S.A.)

   - Say: "Each time our denomination gathers for the national meeting, part of the agenda is the adoption of statements on important issues. These are presented by a committee after a study in which churches can participate and make comments. They are intended to be statements of the delegates to convention on issues of importance to our faith and world. They are one way Baptists take a stand."
   - List the issues from the previous step that created the most discussion.
   - Ask the youth to choose one issue to research and write a statement on.
   - Divide them into small groups or pairs. Let them know that they will be asked to share their work with the rest of the class.
   - List and review the following tasks for them to tackle:
     1. A brief overview of the issue they are addressing.
     2. Appropriate Bible passages to support the position they are taking in their statement.
     3. Specific actions that can be taken by people, churches, and others to do something about the issue.
   - Distribute paper or newsprint to record their work.
   - Give them time to work, circulating to help them as needed.
   - Bring them back together to share their work.
   - Facilitate a discussion using these or your own questions:
     1. Was it easy or difficult to agree about what your resolution should include? Why?
     2. What parts of the statements that were read do you agree with? Disagree with?
     3. Is it easier to just agree with people about what something should say, or is it worth "taking a stand"?

Responding

6. **A song and a prayer.** (5 minutes)
   - Invite the class to sing "Take a Stand!" (If no one knows the tune, read the words from the handout together.)
   - Join in prayer. Ask God for boldness to speak the words God wants us to speak as we take a stand for the gospel.

12

Prophetic Role
Up Against the World—Speaking and Living a Prophetic Word

Bible Basis:
1 Peter 2:1–12

Objectives
At the end of the session youth will be able to:

- compare contemporary standards of living and the way God wants us to live;
- state one way in which they can speak and act as a prophet.

Key Bible Verse:
"You are a chosen race, a royal priesthood, a holy nation, God's own people, in order that you may proclaim the mighty acts of him who called you out of darkness into his marvelous light" (1 Peter 2:9).

Background for the Leader

Christians face a great challenge today—living in a non-Christian world. How do we speak and act as disciples in a culture that is in many ways alien to the gospel? This is a prophetic challenge that involves speaking and living out God's Word so that the world sees, hears, and understands the gospel. Baptists have a long tradition of speaking a prophetic word even when it goes against societal norms. We began by challenging government interference in personal faith, and we continue to apply the gospel to societal issues. In this session we will look at ways Baptists, both as individuals and with others, have played this prophetic role of bringing God's Word to the world.

Baptists were born a prophetic people. From the very beginning they brought God's Word to bear on the significant issues of life.

Baptists began as a people of protest; they stood against the usual and customary ways of thinking and acting. When others believed a civil society was impossible without a state religion, Baptists founded a colony that granted full liberty of conscience in matters of religion. Roger Williams in Providence and John Clarke in Newport were prophets of a new way to understand relationships between the state and the church. This prophetic call was taken up in later times by John Leland in Virginia and Isaac Backus in Massachusetts. It continues to be a Baptist witness today.

While religious freedom was our first, and perhaps greatest, prophetic witness, it is not our only one. Baptists stood tall against the evil of slavery, even though it meant the division of our historic mission societies. Baptists have been prophets of peace in the midst of violence, prophets of justice in the midst of oppression, and prophets of hope in the midst of despair and destruction. Charles Evans Hughes, as secretary of state, and Edwin Dahlberg, as a pastor, were both prophets of peace in the world. Isabel Crawford, as a missionary to the Kiowas, and Walter Rauschenbusch, as a seminary professor and author, were both prophets of social justice. Baptists today continue to proclaim a prophetic message about what it means at the beginning of the twenty-first century to live as people who share the Christian faith.

The prophet's role is not an easy one. It is difficult for the individual, perhaps even more so for a denomination. First, it is a matter of seeking God's word, of discovering what God is saying in a particular time and place about a particular situation or issue. Even if one person has a strong sense of this word, there is still the need to have it tested within the community of faith. For a denomination the process of developing a sense of God's word in the midst of often opposing views is arduous and seemingly impossible. If the word becomes clear, if it is sustained in testing, there still remains the challenge of speaking it clearly and of living it. All of this can drain the spirit of even the most faithful among us.

Despite the difficulties, Baptists continued to assume the prophetic role that comes with being God's people. This is our heritage, a heritage that both challenges and inspires us as we live in a world that continues so often to be at odds with the Good News.

Exploring the Biblical Basis

Early Christians knew what it was like to live in a world that was alien to the gospel, a world in which only a minority professed, shared, and lived by the Christian faith. Living a Christian life put them at odds with all other major religions of the day. Even Judaism, the faith from which they grew, offered hostile opposition to their existence. Yet the Christians continued to proclaim God's Word, to share God's love, and to grow as churches. It wasn't easy. The First Letter of Peter was written to these early Christians in the midst of their struggle and persecution. It offers both encouragement and challenge. In the words of *The New Interpreter's Bible,* ". . . the epistle helps to strengthen Christians in times of distress; sets their lives within the history of God's activity, which moves from creation to consummation; holds up the atoning death of Jesus Christ; and encourages mutual love among Christian people and forbearance of enemies."[1] Peter describes the reality early Christians faced and calls the early followers of Christ to faithfulness.

The passage that is our focus in this session spans two sections of Peter's letter. Verses 1–10 conclude a section that describes God's holy people. Verses 11–12 begin a section on what it means for Christians to live in an alien world of nonbelievers. Thus, we see in it both an affirming description of the faithful and an inspiring challenge to faithful living. This challenge is a call to speak and live a prophetic word.

The passage begins by listing the negative qualities Christians should set aside and describing what they should seek in their lives. Malice, guile, insincerity, envy, and slander are destructive to the community and make growing in faith impossible. They can be countered, much as a mother's milk protects a baby from infection, by "pure, spiritual milk" that enables growth in salvation.

Verses 4 through 8 use the image of "living stones" being "built into a spiritual house" to affirm a close relationship between God's work in Christ and in them. Peter reminds his readers of the ease with which the world rejects the faith, and he encourages them to remain faithful despite rejection. Believers can do this by offering "spiritual sacrifices acceptable to God" and remaining obedient to God's Word.

Verse 9, which is the key verse for this session, boldly affirms who Christians are and what they are to do. Christians are "a chosen race, a royal priesthood, a holy nation, God's own people" so that they might "proclaim the mighty acts" of God. This purpose goes beyond their own salvation; they are called to play a prophetic role for God.

God's mighty acts are not simply what God has done in Jesus Christ, as wondrous as that is. They also include God's continuing work in the world—calling them and us "out of darkness into his marvelous light." That work carries on as others are called to the light as God's love is shared, as God's kingdom comes. This is a biblical warrant for our lives as a prophetic people.

Attempts to respond to God's prophetic call often become divisive within churches and denominations. This passage makes an important affirmation that helps us deal with his reality. It is a theme that runs throughout these verses but is most clearly stated at the beginning: "Rid yourselves, therefore, of all malice, and all guile, insincerity, envy, and all slander." These are words about the way in which members of the Christian community are to treat each other. This theme is picked up again in verses 11 and 12. The "desires of the flesh" are not limited to those of a sensual nature. They include all sins that spring from a focus on self, turning one away from others and from God. This self-centered behavior is precisely that which the author encourages us to set aside in verse 1. The reason for this is clearly stated in verse 12: More than a matter of personal purity, it is so nonbelievers "may see your honorable deeds and glorify God when he comes to judge." The way we treat each other is one of our greatest witnesses to the power of God's love. It is one of the clearest prophetic words we can speak in a world in which love is so often lacking in relationships, especially among those who disagree with each other.

As you prepare for this lesson:

Pray for each youth by name. Denominational life and concerns are probably not a great concern for most youth. As you plan for this session, remember those who will be participating in the class. Consider ways this class can help them to see how the Baptist emphasis

of prophecy relates directly to concerns they face every day. Some may be quite comfortable with a role of being prophets, even among their friends. Others may not have given much thought at all to the prophetic call that comes to all Christians. Remember each student in your preparation prayers. Pray for openness to each other and to the Word of God during this session.

Read and reflect on the Bible passage. Although 1 Peter is less well known than some of the other New Testament epistles, many students will be familiar with the passage that is the basis for this session. Its dramatic imagery makes it perhaps the best-known passage in 1 Peter. The letter itself is not long, so you may want to read it in its entirety. If that is not possible, take time to read 2:1–12 and "Exploring the Biblical Basis" for essential information for your teaching.

Special Materials

- Recent newspapers

Beginning

1. **Share troubling situations.**
   (10–15 minutes)
   - Welcome the youth.
   - Distribute sections of the Sunday morning newspaper or other recent newspapers to the class.
   - Ask them to find articles that illustrate issues or situations they believe Jesus would be concerned about if he were on earth today.
   - Allow several minutes for searching.
   - Ask the youth to share what they have found.
   - After each person shares ask, "What would Jesus do?" (Encourage them to share what they think Jesus would do if he encountered such a situation.)
   - When all have shared, explain that you have been talking about Jesus' role as a prophet.
   - Distribute handout #12.

- Ask the youth to read aloud the description of a prophet: "*A prophet is a person who speaks or acts out God's word for a particular person, time, or place. The gift of the prophet is to discern the way God is at work in the world and to share that with others. This can be related both to a personal issue in someone's life and to important social and/or political issues in society.*"
- Point out that to answer the question, "What would Jesus do?" is to talk about the way in which Jesus would speak or act out God's word for a particular person, time, or place.

Exploring

2. **Learn about Isabel Crawford.** (10 minutes)
   - Say using these or your own words: "We don't ask, 'What would Jesus do?' just because we're curious about Jesus. We ask it to help us live godlier lives. We want to figure out what Jesus would do so that we will know what we should do. In a sense that means that all of us have a prophetic role to play; all of us are prophets."
   - Ask:
     1. Have you ever thought of yourself as a prophet before?
     2. What do you think about this notion?
   - Using material from "Background for the Leader," briefly explain how Baptists throughout our history have played prophetic roles in the world.
   - Tell the class that you are going to take a look at one Baptist who played an important prophetic role early in the twentieth century.
   - Ask them to turn to "Isabel Crawford: A Prophet for Her Time" in the handout.
   - Instruct the youth to put a check mark in the margin next to anything they believe demonstrates the way in which

Isabel Crawford was a prophet. Remind them that it may be either something she said or something she did.
- Ask for volunteers to read one paragraph each.
- Facilitate a brief discussion using these or your own questions:
  1. What did Isabel Crawford do or say that made her a prophet?
  2. How would doing this make you a prophet?
  3. Do you think she did what Jesus would have done in this situation? Why or why not?

3. **Bible study.** (10–15 minutes)
   - Explain that from the earliest days Christians have had a strong sense that to live the way Jesus would live makes us different from the way the rest of the world lives. Note that much of the teaching in the New Testament letters is about this very issue.
   - Ask a youth to read aloud 1 Peter 2: 1–12.
   - Provide background for this passage using the material in the first two paragraphs of "Exploring the Biblical Basis."
   - Tell the youth that the key insights about being a prophet are found in verses 9–12.
   - Divide the class into two groups.
   - Assign one group verses 9 and 10, the other verses 11 and 12.
   - Explain that they are to read their assigned verses and decide what in them provides insight into being a prophet: what a prophet does and why we are to be prophets. Have them use the questions on the handout to guide them in their work.
   - Allow 4 or 5 minutes, then call the groups back together.
   - Ask them to share their insights. (*Material in "Exploring the Biblical Basis" will help you guide this discussion.*)

Responding

4. Decide how to be a prophet today.
(15 minutes)

- Ask youth to brainstorm issues and concerns for which they believe it is most important and/or most difficult to be a prophet today. Write these on newsprint or the chalkboard. *(These may be personal issues having to do with their own lives or broader ones having to do with society. Issues that might be listed here include: drugs and alcohol, sexual activity, treatment of less popular youth, disparity of wealth in the world, violence, ecological concerns.)*

- Ask the class to select one of these to work on together.

- Ask, "What would Jesus do?" *(Remind them that this is in effect asking, "What can we do to act as true prophets in this situation?")*

- As they respond, facilitate a discussion using these or your own questions:
    1. Would doing or saying this be easy or difficult? How?
    2. What would be the consequences of doing or saying this in school? At home?
    3. What if what you do or say doesn't turn out the way you wanted it to?

- If you have time, select another concern and repeat the process.

5. Close with prayer. (5 minutes)

- Summarize by saying something like: "What we've been thinking and talking about is how each one of us can be a prophet. The Bible reminds us that we are aliens and strangers in the world, because the world lives so differently from the way Christians are to live. To be a prophet is to speak and live the way Jesus would even in a world that does not honor that way. We Baptists have a strong tradition of being prophets, just the way Isabel Crawford was a prophet for her day. The challenge for us is to take both our biblical and Baptist tradition and make it come alive in our lives and in our relationships by being prophets ourselves."

- Pray, thanking God for the prophetic witness of those who have come before us. Ask for the strength and courage to live as prophets today.

Note

1. David L. Bartlett, "1 Peter," *The New Interpreter's Bible* (Nashville: Abingdon, 1998), 12:233.

13

Diversity
Different but Together—Celebrate Diversity!

Bible Basis:
Acts 10:34–35; Galatians 3:26–29

Objectives
At the end of the session youth will be able to:

• state the common bond between Baptist churches;
• describe at least two ways Baptist churches are different;
• tell a story about two people who made significant contributions to Baptist life.

Key Bible Verse:
"So there is no difference between Jews and Gentiles, between slaves and free men, between men and women: you are all one in union with Christ Jesus" (Galatians 3:28, TEV).

Background for the Leader

Diversity is and always has been a reality. People are different—in dress, values, skin color, and language. Even Christians have differences. We have a variety of ideas about what meaningful worship is and about the church and its purpose. Every day we are confronted by the differences that abound in the world and are thus challenged to search for common bonds that bring us together. When we find common bonds, it becomes easier for us to affirm our differences rather than fear them. This is true in society. It is also true in the church. Just as there is diversity within churches of different denominations, there is diversity among Baptist churches as well. The purpose of this session is to discover some of the differences that exist and to affirm the common bonds that hold us together. In this way our

differences can be seen more clearly as a source of strength and a reason for celebration.

In the United States racial/ethnic diversity is increasing along with the awareness that diversity exists. The Asian and Hispanic populations of the United States have seen significant growth in recent years, and African Americans and Native Americans play a more significant role in the discussion of what and who our nation is than they did even in the recent past.

These factors have a significant impact on all of us. They make us aware of change and of the fact that change is often difficult to manage. They cause us to wonder what common bonds unite us when the common values, color, and heritage that once held communities together no longer work. They create fear because differences make it more difficult to understand, to communicate, to care.

The other side to this coin of diversity is that as it grows we become more aware of it, and we open ourselves to the possibility of being enriched by the experience and gifts of others. Whether it be something as simple as food or as complex as an understanding of relationships, diversity offers to us the opportunity to learn from each other and grow together.

What is true culturally is also true denominationally. Most Baptist denominations are becoming more diverse. Once predominately white, American Baptist Churches in the U.S.A. may soon be a denomination in which no racial/ethnic group has majority status. Statistics can't tell the whole story, but they do help us begin to see the picture of a new and growing reality. In 1995 resident membership of American Baptist churches was 53 percent Euro-American, 42 percent African-American, 3 percent Hispanic, 1 percent Asian, and .1 percent Native American. Recent years demonstrate a clear trend of a decline in Euro-American members and an increase in all others.[1] This diversity is both a reason for great celebration and a great challenge.

We celebrate the fact that Baptist roots are deeply set in different racial/ethnic communities. All in their own way have found something in being Baptist that enables an important expression of who they are and who they believe God is. We celebrate the fact that Baptists, for a number of reasons but largely because of our historic emphasis on local church autonomy, have long been a diverse group of people. Significant differences have always existed among us, but we still have found ways to be together. We celebrate the richness of our diverse heritage that enables us to enrich our own faith through interaction with and learning from others. We celebrate the great opportunity we have as Baptists to work out our relationships in a context of diversity and recognize that as we do so within the church, we enable it to happen within society.

One challenge we face is to change old patterns in order to enable new relationships.

Another is to continue to affirm the common bonds that unite us even amid great differences. As Christians we must grow together as a whole people of God and not become isolated pockets of homogeneity. We can begin to meet these challenges by becoming more aware and more affirming of the diversity that exists in our own congregations, whether racial/ethnic diversity or diversity of another kind, such as in worship or music styles, theology, age groupings, or something as basic as a difference of opinion about the proper dress for worship. Any diversity calls us as God's people and as Baptists to seek the common bonds that unite us despite our differences and asks us to find an openness to one another that enables us to affirm and learn from our differences.

Exploring the Biblical Basis

In this session we turn to Peter and Paul to discover how they handled the issue of diversity within the early church. The background for Peter's affirmation of Acts 10:34–35 is found in the story that begins with Acts 10:1. Cornelius was a Roman centurion stationed in Caesarea, the Roman headquarters in Palestine. He had shown interest in the Jewish religion and probably had adopted many of their practices, although he had not converted to Judaism. One afternoon he had a vision in which he clearly saw an angel of God and heard the angel direct him to make contact with Peter. He immediately sent his servants in search of Peter. The next day Peter had a vision; this one was a bit more difficult to interpret. While resting on the roof of the house where he was staying, Peter saw what appeared to be a large sheet descending from heaven. In it were a variety of animals that Jews, according to their dietary laws, were not allowed to eat. A voice commanded, "Get up, Peter; kill and eat." Peter protested, knowing that it was against the Jewish law, but the voice continued until the sheet was taken back up into heaven. While Peter pondered the meaning of this vision, word came of the arrival of Cornelius's servants. After hearing their story, Peter went with them to Caesarea, where Cornelius warmly greeted him and described his vision. Peter's reply begins in Acts 10:34–35: "I now realize that it is true that God treats all men alike. Whoever fears him and does what is right is acceptable to him, no matter what race he belongs to" (TEV). The vision was a call to Peter to move beyond the common bond of the law to a new common bond, faith in Christ; to embrace a new diversity of race among God's people.

Paul also dealt with the issue of diversity within the early church. He was the strongest advocate of the mission to the Gentiles. Paul did all he could to incorporate them into the body of Christ without imposing the Jewish law upon them. For Paul, too, there was to be a new common bond, faith in Christ. In the letter to the Galatians, Paul was writing to a church that upset him by listening to a group that claimed followers of Christ must also observe the Jewish law. Throughout the letter he is strong in his condemnation of this view. Repeatedly, Paul sounds the theme of unity in Christ despite social or cultural differences. His strongest affirmation of this view is our passage: "So there is no difference between Jews and Gentiles, between slaves and free men, between men and women; you are all one in union with Christ Jesus" Galatians 3:28 (TEV). In Christ the old distinctions do not disappear; they just don't count for anything anymore. One is still Jew or Greek, slave or free, man or woman, but it doesn't make any difference in the eyes of God or in the eyes of believers. Being together in Christ is such a strong bond of unity that all differences become irrelevant. This becomes the standard by which Christians treat each other.

As you prepare for this lesson:

Pray for each youth by name. Today's class session is about people who are different from us. Differences often prompt interest, but they can also provoke fear. What is different we often do not understand; what we do not understand we often fear. In that fear lies a tendency to view those who are different as wrong or perhaps even as a threat. Youth experience this in a most elemental way in the various cliques of students in their schools. And yet God created the world full of differences so that we might enjoy them and our lives might be enriched by them. Knowing this encourages us to be open to different people, ways, and ideas, even if we may not understand them. Be aware of this tension between fear and openness in yourself and your students as you prepare for this session. Offer a prayer for each of the students as he or she deals with diversity. Pray for help to develop and lead a session that will enable the youth to deepen their appreciation of diversity in their lives, in their community, and in their church.

Read and reflect on the Bible passage. Read both passages that are the Bible basis for this session. Reading Acts 10:1–11:18 as well will give you the full story of Peter and Cornelius and the important role their relationship played in enabling diversity within the early church. If you have time, read the entire Letter to the Galatians. It is only six chapters and provides a wonderful affirmation of the common bond Christians share in Christ, along with stern warnings about falling away from Christ.

Beginning

1. **Differences within the class and church.** (5 minutes)
   - Welcome the youth.
   - Explain that in this session you will be exploring differences within the church. The purpose will be to discover and celebrate the diversity that exists among Baptists.
   - Tell the class that you'd like to begin, not with the church as a whole, but with this class itself.
   - Explain the process: They are to pair up with someone who is different from

them in each of the ways you will name. They will then have a minute to talk with each other about that difference.

- One at a time name a difference (add your own ideas too): hair color, eye color, favorite ice cream, color of skin, best subject in school, etc.
- After their last pairing, ask the group:
  1. Which differences were easier to find a partner for? Why? (Note that some of the ways we are different are visible; others are not.)
  2. Name some other differences among people that are not obvious.
  3. If we're all that different from one another, why are we here together? *(Explore possible answers. Help the class to see that the differences are not as important as what we share in common, which in the church is our belief in Jesus Christ as Lord and Savior.)*

Exploring

2. **Peter and Paul's views on diversity.**
   (10 minutes)
   - Explain that dealing with differences was a major issue in the early church.
   - Share these thoughts in your own words: "Peter and Paul, two of the primary leaders of the church, had to deal regularly with the question of what Christians had in common, what united them despite their differences. They reached pretty much the same answer as we just did. Our belief in Jesus Christ is the most important commonality."
   - Describe the background for Acts 10: 34–35 using the material in "Exploring the Biblical Basis."
   - Ask the youth to turn to the Acts passage and read it.
   - Ask: "In light of what Peter says to Cornelius, what do you think he believed the message of his vision to be?"

- Tell the class that Paul reached the same conclusion when he was confronted with the question of what unites members of a church.
- Use the material in "Exploring the Biblical Basis" to provide the background for the Letter to the Galatians.
- Ask the class to turn to Galatians 3:26–29 and have someone in the class read this passage.
- Ask: "Did Paul really mean there were no differences at all between Jews and Greeks, slaves and free, male and female? If not, what is the meaning of this statement?" *(In the discussion of these passages, help the youth to understand that both Peter and Paul affirm that the common bond for everyone in the church is Jesus Christ. Nothing else is needed. Everything else becomes irrelevant in light of this common bond of Christ.)*

3. **Our diverse Baptist heritage.**
   (25–35 minutes)
   - Explain to the class that just as the early church experienced increasing diversity, Baptists are also a diverse group. You might want to share the statistics about membership that are found in "Background for the Leader."
   - Say: "We are becoming more diverse as a denomination, but there has always been diversity among Baptists. We have a rich heritage of people of different racial/ethnic backgrounds finding a common home among Baptists. One of the important ways of affirming our current diversity as a denomination is to remember the diversity of our heritage. That's what we're going to do now."
   - Divide the class into pairs or small groups.
   - Distribute handout #13.
   - Ask the youth to look at the brief biographies on the handout.
   - Ask: "What do you notice about these

people that make them different?" *(Gender, racial/ethnic diversity: African American, Caucasian, Hispanic, Native American, Asian, etc.)*

- Ask: "What do you notice about these people that makes them similar?" *(They are all Christians. They are all Baptists.)*
- Assign one of these five people to each group.
- Instruct each group to develop a brief presentation (using the handout or additional materials you provided) highlighting the person's significant contributions to Baptist heritage. Encourage them to be creative; they can write a news report or a skit, for example.
- Allow 10 minutes for this work.
- Before bringing them back together, ask the groups to quickly write two multiple-choice questions to ask the class after their presentation. Let them know that it is okay if the incorrect choices they make up are far-fetched. *(The purpose of these questions is to help reinforce the information about the people.)*
- Allow 5 minutes for this work.
- Bring the class back together.
- Ask the youth to share their presentation and questions.
- Conclude this step by referring back to Peter's affirmation of the common bond we share in Christ. Note that this common bond makes the rich diversity of our Baptist heritage possible.

Responding

4. **Celebrate the richness of our Baptist heritage.** (5–10 minutes)
   - Ask the youth to return to the pair or small group they were working in.
   - Ask each group to complete this sentence, which they will share during the closing prayer: "We give you thanks, our God, for (the name of the person whom the group studied), who (list that person's important achievement[s])."
   - Bring the class together.
   - Tell them that each group will read their sentence, and afterwards everyone will respond: "We celebrate the richness of our Baptist heritage!"
   - Gather for prayer. Ask each group to read its sentence and the class to respond.
   - If you have time, close with a song that affirms our oneness in Christ, such as "Bind Us Together, Lord" or "The Bond of Love."

Note

1. Percentages prepared by David Cushman based on the 1995 Annual Reports of the ABC/USA by using simple linear regression with about twenty years of figures from the Congregational Profile System database.

14

Mission
Wherever Love Is Needed

Bible Basis:

Acts 1:6–11

Objectives

At the end of the session youth will be able to:

• describe at least two ways Baptists are witnesses for Christ;

• explain how sharing love with others is a way to be a witness for Christ.

Key Bible Verse:

"'You will be my witnesses in Jerusalem, in all Judea and Samaria, and to the ends of the earth'" (Acts 1:8).

Background for the Leader

Baptists are a mission people: they desire to engage in mission. The realization that the task was too great for any single church led to the beginnings of Baptist denominational life. Churches united, and together they formed the foreign and home mission societies. They worked to publish resources to distribute and to reach people for Christ. This zeal for mission continues. Mission is more than just what national and regional organizations do, however. Because many people do not attend church, America is one of the world's greatest mission fields. Increasingly, the local congregation is seen as a mission outpost.

At one time mission was something that happened "out there"—in the place to which we sent missionaries. We gave our financial support so missionaries could be sent. We listened to the verbal and written reports of the great work made possible because of our giving. But most of the time we had little direct involvement in mission ourselves. "Out there" might be in Africa or Asia, or any foreign land, among people who had not had the opportunity we had to learn about Christ. Or, it might be here in our own country among people who were seen as "needy." Most often, however, we didn't think about mission as happening in our own communities, in our own churches, through our Sunday school and our worship service.

All that has changed. Mission still happens "out there," but now it is clear that it happens, it must happen, "right here," too. We live in an unchurched society. Well over half of our fellow citizens have no significant relationship to a church. Our friends and neighbors, just as much as those halfway around the world, are in need of Christian missionary presence in their lives so they can come to know the saving grace of Jesus Christ.

This means that our understanding of mission—where it happens, how it happens,

63

and who does it—is expanding. Baptist national and regional mission agencies are still vitally important in our worldwide mission effort. They do things no single church could ever accomplish on its own. But now the mission work of the local congregation has taken on new meaning. Virtually every church is a mission outpost in its community, seeking to be a Christian presence in a culture and society that does not know, but needs to know, the Good News.

This expanded understanding of mission has many implications. Denominational structures were created to support mission "out there." Now, structure is needed, both within the denomination and the congregation, to ensure that mission happens "right here" as well. Mission giving used to be something separate from the local budget of the church. Now that distinction is no longer as clear. Money used to support the congregation is as much mission giving as is money sent to support a missionary in another country. Both are important. Both are essential. But this is a different way to think about it.

Mission has always been a driving force in Baptist life. Adoniram Judson, the first Baptist missionary from America, was half way to India before Bible study led him to a belief in believer's baptism. Once Baptists in the United States learned they already had a Baptist missionary on the field, they embraced Judson and his passion for mission. Soon the American Baptist Foreign Mission Society was formed in 1814 to support his work. Similar passion led to the development of the Home Mission Society in 1832. Reaching people for Christ also happens through the printed word and through education. So a passion for mission led to the founding of the American Baptist Publication Society, another mission organization. Over the years, as regional groupings of churches in associations and state conventions developed, a passion for mission led them into important work within their own areas. This same passion for mission is at work in new ways today, with a special focus on the local congregation. Baptists are a missionary people. We always have been, and by God's grace, we always will be.

Exploring the Biblical Basis

The disciples were playing a waiting game. Ever since the amazing day on which Jesus rose from the dead, they had waited—waited for Jesus to appear to them again, waited for the promised coming of God's Spirit. Jesus did come. One last time. They knew it was a special time, and so they asked the question that had been on their minds for days now. "Is this the time you will restore the kingdom to Israel?" In other words, "Is this the time you will make it the way it used to be for us?" Jesus answered by telling them not to worry about time schedules—this was God's concern, not theirs. But then he went on, telling them what they should be doing until God's time was fulfilled. "You will be my witnesses," he said, "in Jerusalem, in all Judea and Samaria, and to the ends of the earth." To paraphrase, "You will be the ones who tell the world about God's work and love, about the great things God has done and continues to do, about the promise God made that can now be claimed by everyone. You will witness to all of that in what you say and in what you do everywhere you go."

Then, ascending into heaven, Jesus left them. And there they stood gazing after him until two messengers from God came along and said, "What are you doing standing here? There's work to be done!"

In this day when the whole notion of what mission is, how and where it happens is being reconsidered, these words of Jesus are especially important for us. Like the disciples, we too, may be longing for past greatness—the way things used to be. But Jesus ignores our concern, not out of callousness, but because he knows there is something more important for us to be about. Instead, he directs our attention to the task at hand—being his witnesses. We start where we are. For the disciples it was Jerusalem; for us it may well be our own community. From there we go where Jesus points the way: to Judea, the surrounding countryside; to Samaria, the neighboring, yet alien and somewhat hostile territory; and on to the ends of the earth. Like the disciples, we may hear these words and be overwhelmed, so much so that we just stand there. We plan but don't move. We talk but don't act. We gaze into the skies wondering what possible difference we can make. But for us, too, there must come the time when we hear the words, perhaps spoken by another, perhaps spoken within our own hearts, "What are you doing standing here? There's work to be done!"

As you prepare for this session:

Pray for each youth by name. This session is about putting our faith into action by becoming involved in mission. It encourages us to move beyond words to actions—both in supporting the mission that is done on our behalf by others and through our own personal involvement. As you think about the members of your class during the week, pray for the mission involvement they already have. They are witnesses for Christ in the different arenas of their lives. Give thanks to God for this mission. Pray that you and they will be open to hearing God's encouraging Word during this class session. Pray that you might be led into fuller participation in God's mission in the world.

Learn about and pray for the mission of Baptists. Our Baptist mission is spread throughout the world, from the work of local congregations to that of missionaries in far-off lands who are supported by denominational structures to the cooperative work of the Baptist World Alliance throughout the world.

Read and reflect on the Bible passage. Read the Bible passage you will be studying. Reflect on the places that are comparable to

Jerusalem, Judea, and Samaria in your life and in the lives of your students. Think about the ways people are and can be witnesses for Christ.

Special Materials

* Recent newspapers

Beginning

1. **Places love is needed.** (5–10 minutes)
   * Welcome the youth.
   * Distribute the newspapers.
   * Explain that the focus of today's sessions is love as a form of mission.
   * Ask the youth to look through the newspapers and cut or rip out articles that describe situations in which love is needed. When all the students have found at least one article, ask them to share their articles and to explain why they chose them.

Exploring

2. **News reports.** (15–20 minutes)
   * Summarize that there are many places where love is needed and that this, at times, can be overwhelming because we might not know where to begin.
   * Divide the class into two groups.
   * Distribute handout #14.
   * Assign one section—"In Thailand" or "In Oklahoma" to each group.
   * Explain that these are two ways Baptists work together to share love.
   * To get the word out, ask the youth to become news reporters. Instruct them to develop a news report—a newspaper article, a television special report, etc.— based on the information contained in the material. Whichever method they choose, remind them to include some first-person comments on the way love is shared and the impact it has on people.

- Bring the class back together when the groups have finished their preparation.
- Ask them to share their reports with one another.

3. **Bible reflection.** (5 minutes)
   - Tell the students that sharing love is one way to understand the mission of the church.
   - Remind them that the church's mission has its foundation in Jesus' last instructions to the disciples.
   - Ask them to turn in their Bibles to Acts 1:6–11, pointing out that this is one record of those last words.
   - Ask a volunteer to read the passage.
   - Note that in naming Jerusalem, Judea, and Samaria, Jesus begins with the place in which they are right then and gradually moves them farther out and away from familiar territory and people.
   - Ask them to turn to "Jesus' Final Words."
   - Give them a couple of minutes to complete the questions.
   - Discuss their answers to the questions. *(These questions are intended to help them respond to the story in a personal way. As they do this they will develop a better understanding of what is going on in the passage. Because the responses are personal, there are no right or wrong answers.)*

4. **Word game.** (5–10 minutes)
   - Write the word *WITNESS* on newsprint or the chalkboard.
   - Tell the class that this is the word Jesus used to describe his followers.
   - Divide the class into two groups, or use the two groups that developed the news reports.
   - Explain that you will be playing a word game. Each team will have a turn to add a word that describes what a witness is or does. The word must connect to one that has already been written. They will take turns until one team is unable to add a word. At that point, if

the other team can add one more word, that team will be the winner. You will be the final authority on whether or not a word is acceptable. Here's an example of the way the game might develop:

```
WITNESS
        EVANGELIZE
    R        O
    V        V
CARE         E
```

- Ask youth to use some of the words listed to write a description of a witness on their handout.
- Ask for volunteers to share what they wrote.

Responding

5. **Where love is needed.** (10 minutes)
   - Give a brief summary of the places in the world that need love, the ways Baptists work to share love, and Jesus' instructions that his followers be witnesses.
   - Say: "Jesus' commandment to begin to witness in Jerusalem speaks of the importance of witnessing in our own communities."
   - Ask:
     1. Which newspaper articles that we looked at relate to our community?
     2. What can you do to share Christ's love there?
     3. Is there anything similar to the situations described in the stories?
     4. What are some other ways in which love is needed?
     5. What are some other ways you can do some of the things that witnesses do that you listed in the word game?
   - Share about the importance of mission involvement "right here," using the material found in "Background for the Leader."

- Remind the class that the need for love is everywhere and that means in their schools as well as in Thailand.

6. **A song and prayer.** (5 minutes)
   - Close with a song, such as "Here I Am, Lord" or "Pass It On." Or choose one that speaks of sharing love or being witnesses for Christ.
   - Pray, thanking God for those who share love in the world. Ask God for strength to be witnesses in our daily lives.

Appendix A
Handouts

Handout #1
Soul Freedom
Who Do You Say Jesus Is?

Bible Basis: Matthew 16:13–16

Key Bible Verse: "'Who do you say that I am?'" (Matthew 16:15).

Soul Freedom

The one place we are always free is in our relationship with God. God made us that way, and there is nothing anyone can do to take that freedom away! That is what soul freedom is all about.

Because Baptists believe in soul freedom, we advocate religious freedom. We were among the very first Americans to support separation of church and state, because we believe that this is the way we can affirm and live out the freedom God has already given us. If the state attempts to tell us what and how and when to pray, it is denying that freedom. But the truth is, we are still free. God made us that way, and not even the government can take away our soul freedom. Without a guarantee of religious freedom, government can make it more difficult for us to practice soul freedom. It can even punish us for doing so, but it cannot take away this freedom.

Soul freedom is also why Baptists believe in believer's baptism rather than infant baptism. If we have soul freedom, then we, not even our parents, are the ones who must decide about our relationship with God. Believer's baptism affirms that only those who are old enough to understand this freedom and use it are old enough to make this important decision about a relationship with Christ. If someone else makes that decision for us, we are not free.

Soul freedom is also the reason for certain differences between Baptists and those of other denominations. We do not have creeds. We believe that each person has the right to determine the precise nature of his or her beliefs and relationship with God, using the Bible as the foundation for these beliefs. Nor do we have bishops. Each congregation is free to make its own decisions about its faith and practice and about what other churches it will relate to. We call this congregational autonomy.

All of these basic Baptist beliefs begin with our belief in soul freedom.

Rights and Responsibilities

Soul freedom isn't just a matter of rights, for with all freedom comes responsibility. Soul freedom isn't simply the freedom to think and believe whatever we want to believe. It's the freedom to develop our relationship with God and to discover God's will and way for our lives—something Baptists believe each person must do for himself or herself. That's why freedom is essential. We also believe that doing so leads to a life of faithfulness to God and to God's Word. The responsibility that goes with soul freedom, then, is the responsibility to develop a relationship with God that is deep and meaningful so that we will discover and follow God's desires for who we will be and how we will live. This can be challenging!

Others Respond to Jesus

Look up the following passages. Consider ways in which soul freedom (the right and responsibility to stand before God and make decisions regarding one's relationship with God) is assumed by the story that is told. You may use the space provided to make notes on each passage.

Mark 1:16–20

• Jesus gave his followers the decision to follow him

Mark 10:17–22

• Mary had to excercise soul freedom in order to decide whether to work with Martha or listen to Jesus.

Mark 14:10–11

• Judas excercised soul freedom when he made the decision to betray Jesus.

Luke 10:38–42

• The man decided that he did not want to put any extra effort to follow God

Soul Freedom Declaration

We believe that we are created by God with the gift of soul freedom.
This freedom gives us the right to:

• Make decisions about our relationship with God
• Choose how and whether to use our talents

This freedom also gives us the responsibility to:

Make decisions about our relationship with God

We believe it is in the exercise of this God-given gift of soul freedom that we develop and live out God's full intentions for us and for our lives.
It's up to us!

Handout #2
Believer's Baptism
Questions That Need Answers

Bible Basis: Acts 8:26–40

Key Bible Verse: "'What is to prevent me from being baptized?'" (Acts 8:36).

Baptist Beliefs about Baptism

Baptists believe in baptism of believers. Baptists believe that when a person is being baptized, he or she is making a statement of his or her belief in Christ as Lord and Savior and of his or her intention to live as a faithful disciple of Christ.

Baptism is possible only after important questions of life and faith have been asked and answered. When a person affirms that the gospel will shape his or her life, that person may be baptized. Because of this, baptism is reserved for people who are old enough to understand and make decisions about important issues.

Baptists affirm baptism as a human response to God's action. God gives us the gift of new life in Jesus Christ; baptism is the sign that we accept that gift. God calls us each day to live lives worthy of the gift we have been given; baptism is the sign that we accept that call. When we are baptized, we declare our faith in God and in God's act of love for us through Jesus Christ. In our baptism, we accept God's daily presence and working in our lives through the Holy Spirit.

Baptists practice baptism by immersion. Baptists immerse the person being baptized in water. The roots of this practice are in the New Testament where the Greek word we translate "baptize" literally means "to dip under." Immersion symbolizes dying to the old life and rising again to new life in Christ. This is the experience of those who seek baptism.

John Smyth and the First Baptists

John Smyth wasn't afraid to speak his mind, even when the consequences were great. In 1602 he was a young preacher at the Anglican Cathedral of Lincoln in England. He stood in his pulpit and told his congregation that the system of priests and bishops of the established church had no foundation in Scripture. *(How do you think that went over?)* This kind of preaching did not sit well with those in power in the church. It wasn't long before John Smyth found himself without a job. Soon, however, a small group of Separatists in Gainsborough called him as their pastor. When persecution of those who were not members of the established English church became severe, Smyth and his congregation moved to Holland. In 1606 they became the Second English Church at Amsterdam.

73

John Smyth kept studying his Bible and kept gaining new understanding of the meaning of Scripture. Two new insights were especially important to him. First, he concluded that the early church was composed only of those who had knowingly repented of their sins, had found forgiveness, and had accepted Christ as Lord and Savior. Second, he concluded that in the New Testament church only those who had first repented of their sins and confessed their faith in Christ were to be baptized.

In 1609 Smyth and thirty-six members of his congregation affirmed that their infant baptism had not been valid. They decided that they must be baptized as believers and that the church should be limited to believers. They dissolved the Second English Church. Smyth baptized himself and then baptized others upon the profession of their faith. Together they formed the first English-speaking Baptist church.

Questions for Reflection

Do you think it would be enough to baptize yourself today? _____ *Why or why not?*

_____

If I were the Ethiopian . . .

Imagine that you are the Ethiopian traveling back home after an important religious experience that has had a deep effect on you. You want to learn more, so you begin to read the Bible. But you don't understand. Suddenly Philip appears and can answer your questions about faith. What would you ask him? Use the space below to write your questions.

- Are end-of-the-world prophecies literal?
- Should the Apochrapha and other "extra" books be included in the Bible?
- Are " " divinely inspired?

If I were Philip . . .

Imagine that you are Philip. You have just encountered the Ethiopian, who is someone you can tell has a deep concern for faith. But he does not yet know much about Christ. What are the things you would most want to tell him about who Christ is and why a commitment to Christ in baptism is important? Use the space below to write notes about these things.

- Christ is Gods' son who died for our sins
- Baptism is important as a commitment to Christ because it follows his example.

Handout #3
The Bible
Read a Good Book Lately?

Bible Basis: 2 Timothy 3:14–17

Key Bible Verse: "All Scripture is inspired by God and is useful for teaching the truth, rebuking error, correcting faults, and giving instruction for right living" (2 Timothy 3:16, TEV).

The Good Book

What's the all-time best-selling book? One of Stephen King's horror novels? Dr. Seuss's *Cat in the Hat*? How about a Shakespeare classic like *Romeo and Juliet*? Wrong, wrong, and wrong again! It's the Bible—the book that has guided Christian believers for generation after generation. Like no other book, the Bible is a source of guidance, encouragement, support, and inspiration for people of all ages. In this lesson we will examine why the Bible is important to all Baptists—including teenagers.

Meet John Smyth

Mention the name John Smyth, and most of us think of the man of Jamestown and Pocahontas fame. But there was another John Smyth whom we rarely read about in history books and don't see featured in Disney movies. This John Smyth was a staunch Baptist minister who felt strongly that there was a right and wrong way to do things. He may not have been much fun at a party, but he was, and still is, well respected for his beliefs. In fact, his contributions to the Christian faith have meaning for us today—nearly four hundred years after his life.

Smyth lived in England in the early seventeenth century. In 1608 he became mired in a controversy with the established church of England over use of the Bible in worship. Smyth felt that translations of the Bible were not the pure Word of God. He insisted that those who led worship must use the original Hebrew and Greek texts, making their own translations for those in their congregations.

As you can guess, Smyth's rigid behavior was not easy for others. "Lighten up," they must have told him. "Chill out." But his desire to be faithful to God's Word had benefits. His ongoing study of the Bible led to two convictions that guided early Baptists and remain important today.

First, Smyth concluded that the hierarchy of the English church, with bishops as mediators between people and God, was unbiblical. A true church, he said, was the gathering of Christian believers in the presence of God's Spirit, joined together in a fellowship of faith. As few as two people, he declared, could comprise a church.

Second, Smyth found that there was no biblical basis for infant baptism. In the New Testament, he said, only those who first asked for forgiveness of sins and declared their faith in Christ were baptized. In 1609 Smyth and thirty-six other members of his congregation—all of whom had been baptized as infants—were rebaptized as believers. Many see this as the first Baptist church ever.

Smyth's convictions about the Bible set the tone for who Baptists are today and for their continued faithfulness to God's Word.

Responding to John Smyth

Complete this sentence and be prepared to discuss your response with the class: I think Smyth's contributions to Baptist life are important today because . . .

_____

Create a Bible Crest

Use the paper your teacher provided to creat a crest that is divided into four quadrants.

1. In the top left quadrant, write the name of a person in the Bible whose life and witness are meaningful to you.

2. In the top right quadrant, draw a favorite biblical symbol (cross, burning bush, rainbow, dove, etc.).

3. In the bottom left quadrant, draw a scene or create a symbol that reminds you of a favorite Bible story or passage.

4. In the bottom right quadrant, write your initials.

Write a Letter

The Bible passage for today's lesson (2 Timothy 3:14–17) comes from a letter written by the apostle Paul to his friend and colleague Timothy. Paul, a first-century missionary, was in a Roman prison awaiting execution for a crime he didn't commit. The purpose of his letter was to encourage Timothy to remain faithful and to remind him to be true to God's Word.

What would you say to a friend or family member (or even yourself) about God's message in the Bible or if you wanted to encourage her or him to read the Bible more often? You may want to reflect on this session's key Bible verse, 2 Timothy 3:16, for ideas. Use a separate sheet of paper to write your letter.

Handout #4
Priesthood of All Believers
But God, I'm Just a Teenager!

Bible Basis: Revelation 1:4–6

Key Bible Verse: "[Christ] loves us and freed us from our sins by his blood, and made us to be a kingdom, priests serving his God and Father" (Revelation 1:5–6).

What's So Special about a Priest?

In the Old Testament priests were a special tribe of Israelites who performed specific religious functions. They were the ones who acted as intermediaries between the people and God. In this role they performed the religious rituals, such as animal sacrifices. They were the only ones engaged in ministry. The great claim of the New Testament is that these roles are no longer limited to a special group of people. They are for everyone. That is what the priesthood of all believers is about.

Priests have access to God. If everyone is a priest, that means everyone has direct access to God. How can we experience that direct access? For ourselves? For others?

Priests have a ministry from God. If everyone is a priest, that means everyone has a ministry. This isn't something just for pastors or others employed by the church. It isn't just for adults. It is for everyone who believes in Christ and is a member of a church. What kinds of ministry are possible for you?

"People Bingo"

Being a priest isn't just about what we do in church. God calls us to live out our priesthood each day—at home, in school, in our neighborhood, even when we are all alone.

Use the Bingo card on the next page to find out how some of your classmates act as priests. Try to get everyone in the class to sign at least one or two squares. Five up and down, across, or diagonally is a winner.

Priesthood of All Believers
BINGO!

B	I	N	G	O
Cheered up a friend who was down	Prayed for a person in need	Read Bible at worship service	Did something to help the poor	Prayed with a friend
Have regular personal devotions	Asked God for forgiveness for something	Went on a mission trip	Shared about Christ with a friend	Forgave someone who hurt you
Spent time in prayer	Asked for God's help in deciding what to do	Prayed for someone who was sick	Thanked teacher for a job well done	Convinced a friend to stop drinking
Stood up for a friend in need	Gave money to a good cause	Helped lead Sunday school class	Volunteered in community	Encouraged a friend to do better
Assisted a neighbor with a chore	Invited a friend to attend church	Befriended a new kid in town	Led a friend to Christ	Apologized to someone you hurt

Are You Up to the Task?

Are you up to the task of being a priest? Respond to the statements below by circling A (Agree), D (Disagree), U (Unsure).

1. It's easy for me to pray to God about my own needs.

    A   D   U

2. I believe I am doing God's work in the world.

    A   D   U

3. I believe God wants me to help others by serving them.

    A   D   U

4. I pray for others and their needs.

    A   D   U

5. I believe it helps other people when I pray for them.

    A   D   U

6. I'm too young to be doing God's work in the world.

    A   D   U

7. God chooses only the best, holiest people to be priests.

    A   D   U

8. I am willing to try to understand what God wants me to do with my life.

    A   D   U

9. I would like to have a deep relationship with God.

    A   D   U

10. I am a priest.

    A   D   U

Questions for Reflection: Write your thoughts.

1. Is it difficult to think about yourself as a priest? Why or why not?

2. What are the things in your life that help you develop a direct relationship with God? What are the things that get in the way?

3. What are some of the ways you think you are doing God's work now? What makes that difficult?

Ready to Be a Priest

Review your answers to the questions in the previous section. Look at the activities that are included in "People Bingo." Then decide on two things you can do to live out your life as a priest more fully. Write them in the space provided below.

I am a priest. I have direct and personal access to God. I am called to be involved in God's work in the world. Because I believe this, I will . . .

1.

2.

Handout #5
Religious Liberty
Free—Even in School!

Bible Basis: Acts 5:17–32

Key Bible Verse: "'We must obey God rather than any human authority'" (Acts 5:29).

Separation of Church and State

Baptists believe that in order for faith to be meaningful it must be free. Separation of church and state is needed so that people can develop their faith and relationship with God free from interference from the government.

Religion and School—Dos and Don'ts

Please write T for TRUE or F for FALSE following each question.

1. Prayer is permitted in public schools.
2. Groups of students may meet for prayer and Bible study in schools.
3. Teachers and other school officials may not lead in prayer at school functions.
4. Schools may not sponsor a baccalaureate service led by community clergy as part of graduation activities.
5. The meaning of Easter and Christmas may be taught in classes.
6. Students have a right to write about their personal religious views in papers and essays.
7. Students may distribute religious literature at school.
8. Student religious clubs may advertise their meetings in the same way non-religious clubs in the school do.
9. Students may wear T-shirts with religious messages and other religious attire.
10. Public schools may not teach a theory of creation based in Genesis as part of their science curriculum.

Religion in Public Schools: What can you do? What can't you do?

Student prayers. You have the right to pray alone or in groups. You may discuss your religious views with peers as long as you are not disruptive. You have a right to read the Bible, to say grace, and to pray before tests. Teachers and school administrators, when acting in their official capacities, cannot encourage or engage in religious activities with students.

They may not include prayer in a graduation ceremony or organize a religious baccalaureate service. If the school rents out its building to private groups, it must rent it out on the same terms to anyone who wants to hold a privately sponsored religious baccalaureate service. The school cannot give preferential treatment to the baccalaureate ceremony. It must be made clear that the school does not endorse the program.

Teaching about religion. Schools can teach you about religion but may not teach religion. The history of religion, comparative religion, and the Bible as literature may all be taught. Schools may teach about explanations of life on earth, including religious ones (such as creationism) in comparative religion or social studies classes. In science class, however, they may present only genuinely scientific critiques of, or evidence for, any explanation of life on earth. Schools may also teach about religious holidays, but they may not observe the holidays as religious events.

Student assignments. You may express your religious beliefs in the form of reports, homework, and artwork. Teachers may not reject or correct your work simply because it includes a religious symbol or addresses religious themes.

Religious literature and dress. You have the right to give out religious literature to schoolmates, subject to reasonable restrictions imposed on the distribution of all nonschool literature. You may wear religious messages on T-shirts as long as other writing on T-shirts is allowed. Students are free to wear religious attire, such as yarmulkes and head scarves. You may not be forced to wear gym clothes that you regard, on religious grounds, as immodest.

Student-led religious clubs. You can organize a student religious club and meet on campus. The club must have equal access to campus media to announce their meetings. Although schools have a right to ban all noncurriculum clubs, they may not single out religious clubs. Teachers may not actively participate in club activities and "nonschool persons" may not control or regularly attend club meetings.[1]

It may be the law, but . . .

It may be the current law, but that doesn't mean everyone agrees with it! Work with your teammates to plan a debate that supports the side assigned to you. Develop your arguments by brainstorming what your debate opponents might come up with and working with arguments to counter them. Use a separate sheet of paper to record the points you'd like to make during the debate and what argument they might counter.

Note

1. This material is adapted from "Religion in the Public Schools: A Joint Statement of Current Law." It and other helpful resources on the separation of church and state are available from the Baptist Joint Committee on Public Affairs, 200 Maryland Ave., NE, Washington, DC 20002. Phone number: 202-544-4226. Internet address: www.erols.com\bjcpa. E-mail address: bjcpa@erols.com.

Handout #6
Autonomy of the Local Church
It's Up to Us to Be the Church

Bible Basis: Acts 2:40–47

Key Bible Verse: "They devoted themselves to the apostles' teaching and fellowship, to the breaking of bread and the prayers" (Acts 2:42).

What Is a Church?

The church is a community of believers.
Baptism is the introductory rite of membership.
Learning, fellowship, worship, and prayer are essential elements of congregational life.
Wondrous things happen within the fellowship of the church.
There is a great intimacy of sharing within the congregation.
As powerful as this community experience is for those who share it, there is always an openness to others, a desire to incorporate new believers whom God provides.

Create a Church

You have the freedom to create a new church from scratch. What would these things be like?

Worship

Music

Prayer life

Leadership

Meetings

The Way People Treat Each Other

Things Church Members Would Do in Your Community

The Way You Feel When You Are Doing Things with the Church

Giving of Time and Money

The Way You Relate to Other Churches

Include anything else that is important to you

What Baptists Think about the Church

Baptists believe that every congregation has the freedom to be the church it believes God has called it to be. And as is always the case, with freedom comes a great responsibility—to listen and respond to God's call to be the church in a particular time and place.

Each Baptist congregation is free to determine its corporate life and its relationships with others. No predetermined hierarchical system dictates to congregations. There are no bishops, no outside controlling groups. Each congregation can set its standards for membership, determine its structure and organization, choose its style of worship.

With this freedom, however, comes the great responsibility of being the church—of listening for and responding to God's call so that the congregation will remain faithful in its life and ministry. No one can tell a local Baptist congregation what it must be and do except God. The congregation's responsibility is to listen and obey when God speaks. Thus, each local congregation needs to *develop a listening stance*, refusing to be so caught up in its own issues and survival that it cannot hear God's voice. It must constantly be *open to change*; *willing to move* in new directions when God calls; and *willing to risk* seeing and doing things differently from others in obedience to God's will. Each congregation must bear its own responsibility rather than relying on bishops or outside structures to tell it how to be faithful. It must claim the responsibility of faithfulness on its own, and that requires the involvement of the people within the church, people like you.

Handout #7
Ministry of the Laity
Someone's Calling

Bible Basis: Ephesians 4:1–7,11–13

Key Bible Verse: ". . . for the work of ministry, for building up the body of Christ . . ." (Ephesians 4:12).

Hopes for the Future

   Please complete the following sentences. It's okay to write the first thing that comes to your mind or to ponder the question and write your best guess.

- Five years from now the most important thing I will be doing is . . .

_____

_____

- Ten years from now I hope that I will be . . .

_____

_____

- Twenty years from now I see myself . . .

_____

_____

Questions for Life

What am I good at?

What do I want to do for the rest of my life?

What makes me really happy?

How can I be successful?

What's special about me?

What is one thing I can do really well?

How important is making a lot of money?

Should I do what other people want me to do?

Does God care what I do?

When God Calls

Moses

Moses was born to Hebrew parents when his people were slaves in Egypt. Because the Egyptian Pharaoh had ordered the killing of all Hebrew baby boys, his mother put him in a basket and hid him among the bulrushes near the river's edge. As fate would have it, he was discovered by the Pharaoh's daughter, who took him home and raised him as her own son. When Moses was a young adult, he came across an Egyptian beating up a Hebrew laborer. In a rage he killed the Egyptian and then fled Egypt. He went to Midian, where he became a sheep herder and got married. All was peaceful until one day when he was out tending the sheep.

Read Exodus 3 and 4. Note especially the way Moses responds to God's telling him to go back to Egypt.

Jeremiah

Jeremiah lived in a time of great difficulty for the people of his country. They were being destroyed militarily from without and disintegrating morally from within. God used Jeremiah to rebuke the people for worshiping false gods. Both the leaders and the common people rebelled against what Jeremiah had to say to them. They became angry and threatened his life on many occasions. And all this had begun one day when Jeremiah had heard a call from God.

Read Jeremiah 1:1–10. Note especially the reason Jeremiah gives for not wanting to respond to God's call and how God deals with that.

Mary

Mary was a young girl who lived in Nazareth. She had just been engaged to an older man, which was not unusual in her day. Back then being engaged involved a legal contract, usually between the man and the woman's father. The engagement period lasted a year, after which the wedding could take place. It was during that year that Mary heard God's call to her.

Read Luke 1:26–38. Note especially how Mary responds to the words of the angel and how the angel responds to Mary.

God's Gifts

Everyone has a gift! One of the basic affirmations of our faith is that everyone has been given at least one gift from God, a gift that makes that person special. How we discover and use our gifts is up to us.

For some people the gift seems obvious. It is something they do well, that they enjoy doing, that people appreciate about them. But that may not really be a gift; it may be a talent or ability rather than a special God-given gift. Often a gift is more difficult to discover—not because it is hidden, but because it is so much a part of us, so natural, that we don't notice it. Or, if we do notice it, we don't think there's anything special about it. A gift is something we don't earn or achieve; it is something that just comes to us. That's one of the reasons we sometimes need other people to help us discover our gifts. We need them to tell us what is special about us!

I think some of my gifts are . . .

God's Call

Once we've discovered our gifts, the next question is, "How are we going to use them?" The answer the Bible gives to that question is, "Doing God's work!" That doesn't mean just being a pastor in a church, or even serving on a board or committee in a church. It might mean that; but it means a lot more as well. God's work is going on everywhere. In order for God's work to get done, many people need to be at work out in the world—in our jobs, in our relationships with others, or in things we do to serve others. Christians believe that God calls each one of us to use our gifts in doing God's work. Most often that call doesn't come through a voice we hear. It comes with an interest, a desire to be involved in something. It could be a feeling that if we don't do something, it just wouldn't feel right. It could be a sense of great happiness or fulfillment we get from doing something. Often, even though we don't hear words, it is like a voice within saying to us, "This is something that's right for you!" When we answer this call we find a deep meaning in life, a meaning that comes from doing the things that God created us for.

Some of the ways God might be calling me are . . .

Some of the places God might be calling me to share in God's work are . . .

Handout #8
Discipleship
Walking and Talking Like Jesus

Bible Basis: Colossians 1:27–29

Key Bible Verse: ". . . to bring each one into God's presence as a mature individual in union with Christ" (Colossians 1:28, TEV).

The Maturity of Jesus

Read the passages below from the Gospel of Luke. Use the space to write the quality of Jesus' maturity that the passage illustrates.

2:41–50

4:1–13

4:16–30

4:42–44

5:27–32

7:11–15

8:22–25

18:15–17

19:1–10

22:28–42

My Discipleship Profile

Complete each section to develop a profile of yourself as a growing disciple of Jesus Christ. A disciple has a *deepening spiritual life.*

The following play an important part in my spiritual life:

Prayer	not at all	some	definitely
Worship	not at all	some	definitely
Bible study	not at all	some	definitely
Meditation	not at all	some	definitely
Service	not at all	some	definitely

A disciple is *being equipped for ministry* through learning and developing skills. God has given me the gifts of:

pastoring: to care, serve, and nurture others	Yes	No	Uncertain
teaching: to help others learn	Yes	No	Uncertain
encouragement: to support others in their growth	Yes	No	Uncertain
sharing: to give generously and naturally	Yes	No	Uncertain
authority: charisma that enables other to follow	Yes	No	Uncertain
kindness: compassion for those in need	Yes	No	Uncertain
wisdom: insight into the meaning of life situations	Yes	No	Uncertain
knowledge: to understand God's Word	Yes	No	Uncertain
faith: deep confidence and trust in God	Yes	No	Uncertain
healing: to bring comfort and wholeness to people and situations	Yes	No	Uncertain
organization: to put things and people together in a way that makes sense and enables them to work productively	Yes	No	Uncertain
inspiration: to lead others to possibilities that exist in them and in situations	Yes	No	Uncertain
creativity: artistic, musical, or dramatic talent	Yes	No	Uncertain
empathy: to listen, understand, and accept	Yes	No	Uncertain
counseling: to help others deal with difficult life situations	Yes	No	Uncertain
communication: talking and writing	Yes	No	Uncertain
envisioning: to see the hidden potential	Yes	No	Uncertain
comfort: to console people in grief and stress	Yes	No	Uncertain
mediation: to bring people together and help them find common ground	Yes	No	Uncertain
apostleship: a deep and evident relationship with Christ	Yes	No	Uncertain
prophecy: to relate the gospel to everyday life	Yes	No	Uncertain
evangelism: to share the gospel with others	Yes	No	Uncertain

others:

Gifts that I want to develop are:

1.

2.

Things I want to learn more about are:

1.

2.

Skills I want to develop are:

1.

2.

Disciples are involved in the ministry of Jesus Christ by serving others in Christ's name.

Ways I serve others are:

1.

2.

Ways I could serve others include:

1.

2.

Steps to Maturity in Jesus

Help me, Jesus, to grow as your disciple by . . .

Help me, Jesus, to strengthen . . .

Jesus, one thing I will do during the coming week to work with you
in a life of discipleship is . . .

Handout #9
Evangelism
Sharing the Good News

Bible Basis: Acts 3:1–16

Key Bible Verse: " 'I have no silver or gold, but what I have I give you; in the name of Jesus Christ of Nazareth, stand up and walk' " (Acts 3:6).

Good News Is for Sharing!

This is a conviction that Christians have held ever since Jesus' resurrection. It was good news—and this good news was to be shared! Today's lesson challenges us to think about ways to share the Good News of Jesus with others.

Sometimes we refer to the Bible as the Good News. Briefly write out the "good news" story of Jesus Christ.

What Is Evangelism?

The American Heritage College Dictionary says that evangelism is:

1. Zealous preaching and dissemination of the gospel, as through missionary work.
2. Militant zeal for a cause.

Baptists have a definition too! Here it is:

Evangelism is
  the joyous witness of the People of God
    to the redeeming love of God
  urging all to repent
  and to be reconciled to God and each other
  through faith in Jesus Christ
    who lived, died, and was raised from the dead,
so that
    being made new
    and empowered by the Holy Spirit

believers are incorporated as disciples into the church
  for worship, fellowship, nurture and
    engagement in God's mission
      of evangelism and liberation within society and creation,
    signifying the Kingdom which is present and yet to come.[1]

Seven Essential Points about Jesus

When telling the story about the Good News of Jesus Christ, biblical scholars say there are seven essential points one could make. As you look at this list, note in the space provided which of these points you could hear yourself saying to a friend. Note also how you might restate the point in a way you would feel comfortable and in a way you think she or he could hear it.

1. God sent Jesus as a special messenger to reveal God's love to us.
2. Jesus, God's Son, is fully God, yet he lived on earth fully as a human being as well. Jesus, *"the two-hundred percent person!"*
3. Jesus, God's only Son, the best gift God could offer, was rejected.
4. Jesus, the one who leads people to life, was put to death.
5. But on the third day, God raised him from death to life, just as the prophets foretold.
6. When we put our faith in Jesus, we are empowered by the Spirit of God to live abundant lives in his grace and in service to humanity.
7. We are witnesses to his resurrection, and we are now compelled to share this very good news with everyone we possibly can![2]

Use the space below to note the name or names of people with whom you would like to share the Good News of Jesus Christ.

One thing I most want to tell them about the Good News of Jesus Christ is . . .

Each day this week pray for the name(s) on your list. Pray for the words and the courage to share the Good News. Ask God to guide you to a time and place where you can share with your friend(s) your joy in knowing Jesus! And thank God for the privilege of having such a great story to share.

God bless you!

Notes

1. American Baptist Policy Statement on Evangelism, adopted June 1984.
2. Paraphrase and adaptation of C. H. Dodd, *The Apostolic Preaching and Its Developments: Three Lectures, with an Appendix on Eschatology and History* (New York and London: Harper & Brothers, 1936; reprint 1949), 17.

Handout #10
Worship and Communion
Dead or Alive?

Bible Basis: Psalm 95:1–7a

Key Bible Verse: "O come, let us worship and bow down, let us kneel before the LORD, our Maker!" (Psalm 95:6).

Psalm 95

¹O come, let us sing to the LORD;
let us make a joyful noise to the rock of our salvation!
²Let us come into his presence with thanksgiving;
let us make a joyful noise to him with songs of praise!
³For the LORD is a great God, and a great King above all gods.
⁴In his hand are the depths of the earth;
the heights of the mountains are his also.
⁵The sea is his, for he made it,
and the dry land, which his hands have formed.

⁶O come, let us worship and bow down,
let us kneel before the LORD, our Maker!
⁷For he is our God,
and we are the people of his pasture,
and the sheep of his hand.

Creating a Worship Experience

Here's a worship outline. Use the suggestions or add your own ideas to fill in the blanks. Keep in mind the qualities you talked about that makes worship come alive for you.

Call to Worship

Psalm 95 invites people to worship, which is what a call to worship is all about. In the space below write your own version of the psalm. Use ideas and images that mean something in today's world and to you personally. What specific things has God done that you want to mention (other than making the dry land)? What ways can you talk about who God is (other than rock and shepherd)? Use these things as the basis for your psalm.

96

Song of Praise

To get worship off to the right start, it is important to focus on God. A song of praise for who God is and what God has done or that celebrates God's creation is often used to do this. What songs do you like that could be used to do this?

Prayer

Prayer serves many functions in a worship service. It offers thanks for God's gifts to us, provides an opportunity to ask for forgiveness, asks for God's involvement in our personal needs, and lifts others and their needs to God. In the space below write your own thoughts in each of these areas, then put them together in a prayer. Remember though, your prayer isn't just for you; it is for your entire class.

I'm/We're thankful to God for . . .

I/We need to ask God's forgiveness for . . .

I/We need to ask God's help in . . .

I/We want to ask God's support for . . .

Hearing God's Word or "The Message"

One way to relate God and God's Word to our own lives and the lives of others is to think about the specific hurts and hopes we have. It is then possible to turn to the Bible to discover ways in which it speaks to these. Use the space below to record hurts and hopes that are important to you and to others in your class.

Some important hurts are . . .

Some important hopes are . . .

Now use your own knowledge of the Bible, or a topical concordance if one is available, to discover Bible passages that speak to one of the hurts or hopes. Here are a few suggestions of passages that may help as well: family relationships—Luke 15:11–32; anger—Matthew 5:21–26; Ephesians 4:25–5:2; James 1:19–27; forgiveness—Matthew 6:14–15; 18:21–35; Colossians 3:12–14. Decide on a way to present this passage to the class. You might do a contemporary version of it as a skit. You might read and act it out in a dramatic way.

Communion

The celebration of Communion is based in Jesus' experience with the disciples at the Last Supper. Read Luke 22:14–20 and 1 Corinthians 11:23–26 for descriptions of that experience that the early church used as the basis for Communion. Key words related to this experience are: *remember, sacrifice, forgiveness, unity, special sense of Christ's presence.* Use these to develop a brief statement inviting people to join at the Communion table. If you will share Communion as a class, use the words related to the sharing of the bread and cup that are found in 1 Corinthians 23–25. If your class will not be sharing in Communion, use the invitation you write as a statement about the meaning of Communion.

Song of Affirmation or Commitment

At the conclusion of worship it is important to think about what difference the experience will make in our lives. A song that affirms the message of the service or encourages us to act on that message helps do this. Select a song you like that will serve this purpose.

Handout #11
Issues of Faith
Take a Stand!

Bible Basis: Acts 4:23–31

Key Bible Verse: "When they had prayed . . . they were all filled with the Holy Spirit and spoke the word of God with boldness" (Acts 4:31).

Take a Stand!

Does it matter if I run, or stand?
Does it matter if the world just circles all around me?
What if I don't do my part?
Do you really think it makes a difference what I do with my life?

> Take a stand. Do your part.
> Reach out to ev'ry heart,
> May the Christ within help us see.
> We're working in the night, we can be a holy light
> If we'll take a stand and live what we believe.
> Take a stand.

The world is in need of hope;
Looking all around for something to believe in.
Will we share the truth we know?
The thing that makes all the difference is the Christ in our lives.

Yes, it matters if we run or stand.
Let's not let our world just circle on around us.
If we each will do our part
Christ can make all the difference in the lives that we touch.[1]

Amos: Up Close and Personal

Amos was a herdsman who became a prophet in Israel about 750 years before Jesus was born. The society Amos saw and spoke about was one in which:

- there were a few very wealthy people
- many people struggled just to get by
- the gap between rich and poor was growing greater
- the rich had every luxury the world of that day could provide

- the poor didn't have enough to eat
- government officials were easily and often bribed by those who had the money to do so
- the rich foreclosed on the property of the poor, leaving them with no way to make a living
- the rich continued to worship at the temple and observe other religious feasts but seemed to have no concern for the poor

List some similarities and differences between then and now.

Should We Take a Stand?

For each of the following issues put a check on the line if you believe God wants you and/or the church to take a stand:

	Me	The Church
The poverty in our nation when some people are so wealthy	____	____
The poverty of Third Word nations when our country is so wealthy	____	____
Abortion	____	____
Issues of sex and sexuality	____	____
Racism	____	____
Sexism	____	____
Supporting specific people for election to office, such as president, senator, or governor	____	____
Prayer in public schools	____	____
Assisted suicide	____	____
The death penalty	____	____
Terrorism	____	____
Intolerance for people of different faiths	____	____

Note

1. *Take a Stand! 23 Songs to Make a Better World*, Better World Artists and Activists Guild and American Board of Education and Publication, 1996.

Handout #12
Prophetic Role
Up Against the World—Speaking and Living a Prophetic Word

Bible Basis: 1 Peter 2:1–12

Key Bible Verse: "You are a chosen race, a royal priesthood, a holy nation, God's own people, in order that you may proclaim the mighty acts of him who called you out of darkness into his marvelous light" (1 Peter 2:9).

What Is a Prophet?

A prophet is a person who speaks or acts out God's Word for a particular person, time, or place. The gift of the prophet is to discern the way God is at work in the world and to share that with others. This can be related both to a personal issue in someone's life and to important social and/or political issues in society.

Isabel Crawford: A Prophet for Her Time

Isabel Crawford was born in Ontario, Canada, in 1865. She was the daughter of a Baptist minister who served churches in both Canada and the United States. A severe childhood illness left her deaf. At age eleven she had a conversion experience. This led her to have a deep concern for others, especially the poor of the cities.

When Isabel graduated from Baptist Missionary Training School, she expected to be appointed to city mission work. The appointment that came, however, was to work among Native Americans in Oklahoma. By her own account, she cried for several days after receiving the news but then determined that, if this was God's will, she would go and devote herself to the work.

Isabel's first position was on a reservation eighty-seven miles from the nearest railroad. Within a few years she moved to an even more isolated place called Saddle Mountain. There she began her most significant work. She shared the gospel, her possessions, and herself to bring the love of Christ to those she came to love. She began a church and led in the construction of a church building. Believing that all Christians were called to give to others, she began a missionary society that would support other mission work. When government supplies failed to arrive on time, she became an articulate and forceful advocate for the Native American cause.

Isabel's ministry among the Kiowas ended in controversy. The church was located far from any ordained clergy. On one Communion Sunday, at her suggestion, the church voted unanimously to let a Native American church leader, Lucius Aitson, preside at the Communion service. Affronted by this decision, the pastors of the local association adopted a resolution of censure. The church was reported to the Home Mission Society and threatened with expulsion from the association. To avoid further conflict, Crawford resigned her position and ended her ministry with the Kiowas. The remainder of her life was spent in mission and deputation work. When she died in 1961 her body was returned to Saddle Mountain. Her grave is marked with the simple inscription, "I dwell among my own people." The one whom the Kiowas called a "Jesus Woman" and named Geehhoangomah, "She gave us the Jesus way," had come home.

Insights on Being a Prophet

What insights are provided by 1 Peter 2:9–10?

What do these terms mean to you:

A chosen race _____

_____

Royal priesthood _____

_____

A holy nation _____

_____

God's own people _____

_____

What do these terms mean for the way Christians are to live?

What is meant by the phrase "proclaim the mighty acts of him who called you out of darkness into his marvelous light"?

How might you do that?

What insights are provided by 1 Peter 2:11–12?

In what ways were early Christians aliens and strangers (v. 11)?

In what ways are you an alien and stranger in today's world?

Desires of the flesh (v. 11) is about more than sex. It refers to all sins that spring from a focus on ourselves, turning us away from others and from God. What do you think some of these might be? (Check out 1 Peter 2:1 for a clue.)

Why should Christians "conduct themselves honorably" (v. 12)?

Handout #13
Diversity
Different but Together—Celebrate Diversity!

Bible Basis: Acts 10:34–35; Galatians 3:26–29

Key Bible Verse: "So there is no difference between Jews and Gentiles, between slaves and free men, between men and women: you are all one in union with Christ Jesus" (Galatians 3:28, TEV).

Lulu Fleming

For Lulu Fleming, accepting Christ was much more than being a believer. Along with the acceptance of Christ came acknowledgment of a responsibility to teach others about Christ so that they might be free through his salvation. When the Woman's American Baptist Foreign Mission Society asked for women to serve as missionaries, Lulu knew she was called. In 1886 she became the Society's first woman of African descent commissioned for missionary service.

Lulu was a native of Florence, Florida. Her grandfather had been brought to America from the Congo. She was born into a poor slave family. Her father, though he was a slave, left his family to fight in the Union army during the Civil War. Once the bells of freedom rang after the war, Lulu, with help from her mother, received an education. This led to a brief time of public school teaching, then to college and seminary.

After her commissioning Lulu set sail for her assigned mission field in the Congo. Once there she taught school, but her strongest desire was to be free to do town and jungle work, evangelizing men and women. Illness brought her back to the United State in 1891 after four years in the Congo. She brought with her several Congolese students and helped them to attend Shaw University, her alma mater. While in the United States she studied medicine.

In 1895 Lulu returned to the Congo as a medical missionary, but she was soon stricken with "sleeping sickness," which forced her to return to the United States. She died in 1899, soon after her return.

Jitsuo Morikawa

Jitsuo Morikawa was born in British Columbia on May 1, 1912. He moved to the United States for his education and received a bachelor of divinity degree from Southern Baptist Seminary in Louisville, Kentucky. During World War II he spent eighteen months in the Poston Relocation Center with other Japanese Americans who were placed there simply because of their race. Later he said that the faithfulness of his own denomination and that of the American Friends Service Committee in championing the cause of Japanese Americans made an unforgettable impact upon his life and future ministry.

Following his forced relocation to Poston, Morikawa spent twelve years as pastor of the First Baptist Church of Chicago. There he directed the church's involvement in the first major urban renewal program in America. He later served as director of evangelism for American Baptists. He was one of the denomination's best-known and best-loved leaders. But he was also a controversial figure, largely because of his quiet and intellectual nature and his belief that the gospel had direct meaning for social and political issues. Morikawa believed that institutions, like individuals, sin and therefore need to be converted to Christ.

After his retirement from denominational leadership, Morikawa served as pastor of several churches. He died in July 1987 at the age of seventy-five.

Walter Rauschenbusch

Walter Rauschenbusch was born in 1861, the son of a minister, sixth in a line of ministers. He became a committed Christian at about age sixteen. Soon after, he decided to study to become a minister. Originally he had hoped to be a foreign missionary, but his application was turned down because, unknown to him, his Old Testament professor considered Rauschenbusch's views of the Old Testament "too liberal" and intervened in the selection process to prevent him from becoming a missionary.

In 1889 Rauschenbusch was called to the Second German Baptist Church in New York City. This church was located in a part of the city known as "Hell's Kitchen" because of the crime, poverty, and disease so prevalent there. He served the church for eleven years. During this time he began to envision a program for social action based in the gospel. This was in a very real sense a second conversion experience for Rauschenbusch. In it he gained a radically new outlook on the meaning of the gospel and the kingdom of God.

Rauschenbusch found in the Bible a deep compassion for the oppressed by a God who stood for justice and righteousness. With this came a calling to minister not only to the individual, but also to society as a whole.

In 1897 Rauschenbusch joined the faculty of Rochester Seminary, which is now Colgate Rochester Theological Seminary. There he further developed his ideas. He shared them with students through his teaching and with others through his writing. Rauschenbusch died in July 1918, just as World War I was drawing to a close. As he felt death approaching from a fatally progressive cancer, he said, "I am sorry to be leaving a world where there is so much hate and to be going to a country where there is so much love." He realized that there was and is still much work to be done.

Concepcion Renteria

Concepcion Renteria was commissioned as a missionary of the Woman's American Baptist Home Mission Society in October 1887. At the time she was about sixty-five years old. Although she was not associated with the society until late in her life, she was involved in missionary work in Mexico for a long time.

Concepcion received no formal training for her mission work. She was, however, exceedingly capable. She described her work this way: "Each day I go out to my visits from house to house, in which I usually find persons that with pleasure hear the Word of God. In some houses gather from nine to ten persons…. Every week I hold a meeting at my house to read the Bible and have a prayer, after which we take a collection to help Mexican missions…. We had seven baptisms this month, and one of them is a young lady from the Sunday school. All here persist in telling me to remain a long time. Every day I have greater hope and work. I have visited many people, and great revival rejoices me."

Concepcion's mission was so successful that she was asked to expand her work. Soon she was moved to the mission school in Monterey, in part to fill a vacancy there and in part to recover from an intermittent fever that afflicted her. She was a powerful preacher with a simple faith and a zealous heart. She shared her faith wherever she went, even while traveling on the train between cities.

Concepcion retired from active missionary work in July 1892 and died in October 1893.

Jesse Bushyhead

By the 1840s the American Baptist Home Mission Society was maintaining over a dozen Native American missions, with twelve churches, six schools, and twenty-eight missionaries. One of these was with the Cherokees, who had been forcibly removed from their home in the Carolinas, Georgia, Alabama, and Tennessee and resettled in Oklahoma. Although directed by a white missionary, part of the work was handled by four Cherokee preachers. One of these was Jesse Bushyhead. He had been among the leaders who developed the constitution of the Cherokee Nation and served for many years as chief justice of the Cherokee Supreme Court. As a missionary he rode a circuit of 240 miles, ministering to people who, as he wrote, were "flocking to hear the word of God preached or read." An important part of his work was translating the Bible into Cherokee. When he died, he had just finished translating the Book of Genesis.

Handout #14
Mission
Wherever Love Is Needed

Bible Basis: Acts 1:6–11

Key Bible Verse: "You will be my witnesses in Jerusalem, in all Judea and Samaria, and to the ends of the earth" (Acts 1:8).

In Thailand

Kim Brown, an American Baptist missionary in Thailand, shares the following story:

As a young girl in northern Thailand, NaUr was abandoned by her parents. At age thirteen she was forced to marry an older man. A year later she gave birth to a premature child who died within minutes. Her husband left her, and at age fifteen relatives sold her to a brothel owner. After a year of shame and agony, she escaped and returned to her village only to be sold again into prostitution.

About a year later, NaUr became ill. The brothel owner waited four months to send her to a hospital. After three days, hospital officials contacted the Health Project for Tribal People (HPTP) directed by American Baptist missionary Kim Brown. HPTP had expanded its ministry of AIDS education weeks earlier by opening House of Love, a home for HIV-infected women and their children.

NaUr became their newest resident. She arrived too weak to sit. She was malnourished and suffered from pneumonia, tuberculosis, and severe abdominal cramps. Her breathing was labored. She had AIDS—and was lonely and frightened.

Within days NaUr's temperature soared, and she was admitted to a nearby hospital. Says Brown, "As I sat at her bedside holding her hand, I kept thinking how terrible it must be to die having never known that you were loved or cared for by anyone. I began to cry thinking about her short life and how very alone she must have felt. I prayed that she would recover enough that she could … experience what it meant to be loved and cared for."

Before she could return to the House of Love, NaUr died. She was nineteen. She did experience God's love during her final days on earth. House of Love staff members took turns visiting NaUr, sitting with her, holding her hand, and sharing comforting words of the gospel. At the House of Love, residents experience love—often for the first time.

In Oklahoma

Joan Brown, director of Murrow Indian Children's Home, shares the following story:

Recently several young people living at Murrow Indian Children's Home, a mission partner of American Baptist National Ministries, dedicated their lives to Christ and were baptized. Candace was the first to make her decision. She is thirteen years old and had been abused and neglected by her parents. She and her brothers and sisters had not attended school regularly, and Candace has not really gone to school since the fourth grade. She is now in seventh grade and struggling to keep up. She desperately wants to pass and continue on with her school friends.

The staff at Murrow is very proud of Candace, and we are working to encourage and support her. She works with the tutor every day while the other children are playing after school. We wonder sometimes how it is that the children are not attending school and parents are not held accountable. Too many times minority children are ignored or overlooked by the authorities, and the children suffer.

Karaina, age sixteen, was sexually abused by her stepfather. One of her older sisters has a baby by this man. Their mother worked two jobs to support the family and would not acknowledge the abuse; she herself has a history of abuse. The father is now in prison. A new Christian and a beautiful young woman, Karaina prays for strength and the ability to help others who have suffered as she has.

Jesus' Final Words

Read Acts 1:6–11, then select what you believe is the best completion for each of these sentences. Discuss your choice and the reasons for it with your class.

1. The disciples wanted Jesus to restore the kingdom to Israel because
   ____ they wanted to get rid of the Roman army that was occupying their country.
   ____ they believed the only way God could rule was through a national government.
   ____ they wanted to be the rulers of the restored Israel.
   ____ they wanted to recapture the glories of the past, such as when David and Solomon ruled Israel.

2. Jesus told them, "It is not for you to know the times and dates" because
   ____ he thought it was none of their business.
   ____ he didn't know either and didn't want to answer.
   ____ he believed there were more important things for them to be thinking about.
   ____ there are some things that humans shouldn't know about God's plan for creation.

3. If Jesus were speaking to your class right now, what places would he name instead of "Jerusalem, Judea, Samaria and to the ends of the earth"?

   Jerusalem: _____

   Judea: _____

   Samaria: _____

4. If I had seen Jesus taken up into heaven, I
    _____ wouldn't believe it.
    _____ would be convinced that he truly was the Messiah.
    _____ would be afraid not to do everything he told me to do.
    _____ would be so shocked I couldn't think or do anything.

5. The two men came to the disciples
    _____ to tell them to quit standing around and get to work.
    _____ to reassure them that they would see Jesus again.
    _____ to remind them that they would need to get by without Jesus now.
    _____ to fill them in on details about Jesus' return.

Witness

Write what a witness does, in your own words. It is okay to use words from the witness word game.

List at least two ways you can be a witness for Christ.

1.

2.

Appendix B
Baptist Heritage Resources

Brackney, William H. *Baptist Life and Thought: A Source Book*. Revised. Valley Forge, PA: Judson Press, 1998.

Uses primary documents from the seventeenth through the twentieth centuries to provide insight into important Baptist beliefs.

Celebrate Freedom! Macon, GA: Smyth and Helwys, 1998.

A Vacation Bible School curriculum based on important Baptist principles.

Freeman, Curtis W., James Wm. McClendon, Jr., and C. Rosalee Velloso da Silva. *Baptist Roots: A Reader in the Theology of a Christian People*. Valley Forge, PA: Judson Press, 1999.

Primarily an examination of baptist theology, this study contains selected and excerpted historical documents relevant to the development of the baptist movement and of Baptist denominations.

Goodwin, Everett C. *Baptists in the Balance: The Tension between Freedom and Responsibility*. Valley Forge, PA: Judson Press, 1997.

A collection of essays, sermons, lectures, and articles that reflect a variety of perspectives on Baptist life in the late twentieth century.

Jones, Jeffrey D. *Keepers of the Faith: Illustrated Biographies from Baptist History*. Valley Forge, PA: Judson Press, 1999.

One-page stories of eighty important Baptists told through captioned illustrations. Can be reproduced for use as bulletin inserts or handouts.

Maring, Norman H., and Winthrop S. Hudson. *A Baptist Manual of Polity and Practice*. Revised. Valley Forge, PA: Judson Press, 1991.

Draws on New Testament and historical sources to explore practical implications of the Baptist understanding of the church.

Our American Baptist Heritage. Video series.

A four-part video series on important events and people in American Baptist Life: The First Baptists, Baptists in Early America, Unity and Diversity in the American Baptist Movement, American Baptists Come of Age. Call 1-800-4-JUDSON to order. Valley Forge, PA: Board of Educational Ministries, n.d.

People with a Mission. Video.

A video version of a classic filmstrip that tells the story of American Baptists. A script for use with children is also available. Call 1-800-4-JUDSON to order. Valley Forge, PA: Board of Educational Ministries, n.d.

Proclaiming the Baptist Vision. Edited by Walter Shurden. 4 volumes. Macon, GA: Smyth and Helwys, 1993.

Four separate volumes of sermons: *The Bible, The Church, The Priesthood of All Believers, Religious Freedom*.

Shurden, Walter. *The Baptist Identity: Four Fragile Freedoms*. Macon, GA: Smyth and Helwys, 1993.

Explores historical origins and contemporary meaning of Bible, soul, religious, and church freedom. Leader's guide available.

Skoglund, John. *The Baptists*. Valley Forge, PA: Judson Press, 1967.

A booklet that provides a statement of commonly accepted Baptist doctrines.

Torbet, Robert G. *A History of the Baptists*. 3d ed. Valley Forge, PA: Judson Press, 1963.

A classic and comprehensive history of Baptists.